THE BOOKLOVER AND HIS BOOKS

THE BOOKLOVER AND HIS BOOKS

HARRY LYMAN KOOPMAN, Litt.D.

GYAN

Published by

Gyan Publishing House
5, Ansari Road
Daryaganj, New Delhi-110002
Phone: 011-47034999, 9811692060
E-mail: books@gyanbooks.com

Distribution Network
gyanbooks.com
India, USA, Canada, UK, Australia, France

ISBN : 978-81-212-9244-3 (PB)
First Published, 1917

2nd Impression 2023

Printed at: Gyan Press, Delhi.

THE BOOKLOVER AND HIS BOOKS
Author: HARRY LYMAN KOOPMAN

THE BOOKLOVER AND HIS BOOKS

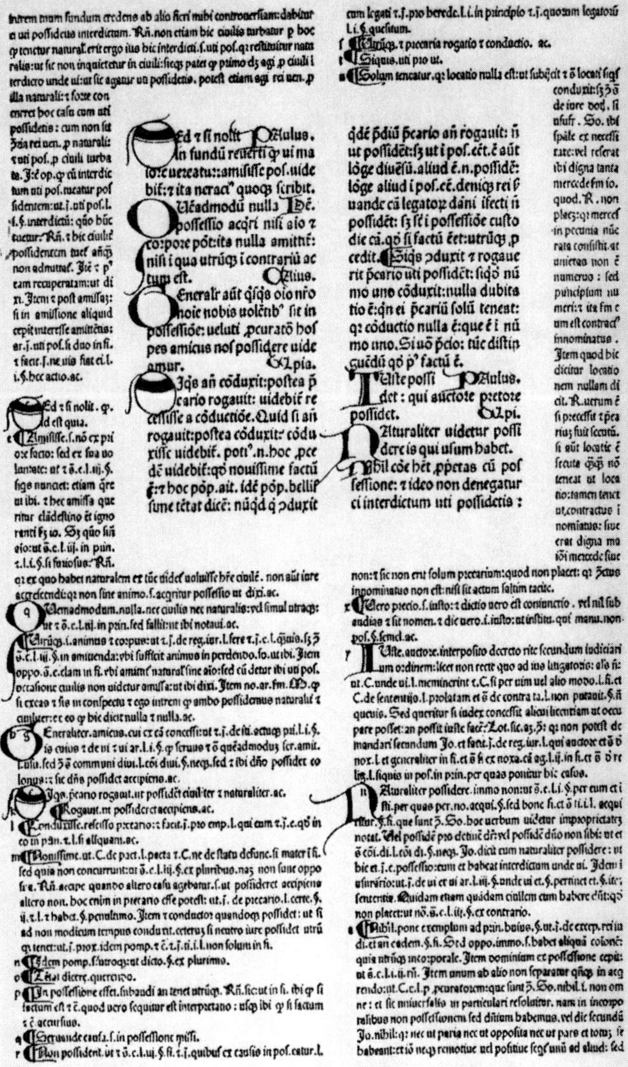

Sed et si nolit [P]aulus.
in fundū reuerti q̄ ui ma
ioꝛe uerea[tur]: amisisse pos. uide
bit: et ita nerac[ius] quoq; scribit.
[Q]uēadmodū nulla [I]dē.
possessio acq̄ri nisi aīo et
coꝛpore pōt: ita nulla amittit:
nisi i qua utrūq; i contrariū ac
tum est. [C]elius.
[G]eneralr aūt q̄sq̄s oīo nr̄o
noīe nobis uolētib[us] sit in
possessiōe: ueluti ꝓcuratō hos
pes amicus nos possidere uide
amur. [V]lpia.
[S]Iq̄s añ cōduxit: postea p̄
cario rogauit: uidebit re
cessisse a cōductiōe. Quid si añ
rogauit: postea cōduxit: cōdu
xisse uidebit. poti[us].n. hoc ꝓce
dē uidebit: qd̄ nouissime factū
ē: et hoc pōp. ait. idē pōp. bellis
sime tētat dicē: nūq̄d q̄ ꝯduxit

q̄dē ꝑdiū p̄cario añ rogauit: n̄
ut possidēt: s; ut i pos. eēt. ē aūt
lōge diuēsū. aliud ē.n. possidē:
lōge aliud i pos. eē. deniq; rei s̄
uande cā legatoꝝ dāni īfecti n̄
possidēt: s; sē i possessiōe custo
die cā. qd̄ si factū ēet: utrūq; ꝓ
cedit. [S]iq̄s ꝯduxit et rogaue
rit p̄cario uti possidēt: siq̄d nū
mo uno cōduxit: nulla dubita
tio ē: q̄n ei p̄cariū solū teneat:
q: cōductio nulla ē: que ē i nū
mo uno. Si uō p̄cio: tūc distin
guēdū qd̄ p[ost] factū ē.
[T]Uste possi [P]aulus.
det: qui auctore p[r]etore
possidet. [V]lpi.
[N]Aturaliter uidetur possi
dere is qui usum habet.
[N]ihil cōe hēt ꝓpetas cū pos
sessione: et ideo non denegatur
ei interdictum uti possidetis:

From the *Digestum Novum* of Justinian, printed at Venice by Jenson in 1477.
The type page of which this is a reduction measures 12½ by 8½ inches.
The initials in the original have been filled in by hand in red and blue.

From the copy in the Library of Brown University

THE BOOKLOVER AND HIS BOOKS

BY

HARRY LYMAN KOOPMAN, Litt.D.

LIBRARIAN OF BROWN UNIVERSITY

BOSTON

THE BOSTON BOOK COMPANY

1917

TO
THE AUTHORS AND THEIR PRINTERS
WHO HAVE GIVEN US
THE BOOKS THAT WE LOVE

PREFATORY NOTE

THE following chapters were written during a series of years as one aspect after another of the Book engaged the writer's attention. As they are now brought together, the result is not a systematic treatise, but rather a succession of views of one many-sided subject. In consequence there is considerable overlapping. The writer hopes, however, that this will be looked upon not as vain repetition but as a legitimate reinforcement of his underlying theme, the unity in diversity of the Book and the federation of all who have to do with it. He therefore offers the present volume not so much for continuous reading as for reading by chapters. He trusts that for those who may consult it in connection with systematic study a sufficient clue to whatever it may contain on any given topic will be found in the index.

Most of these chapters appeared as papers in "The Printing Art"; two were published in "The Graphic Arts," and some in other magazines. The writer expresses his thanks to the proprietors of these periodicals for the permission to republish the articles in their present collective form. All the papers have been revised to some extent. They were originally written in rare moments of leisure scattered through the busy hours of a librarian. Their writing was a source of pleasure, and their first publication brought him many delightful associations. As they are presented in their new attire to another group of readers, their author can wish for them no better fortune than to meet — possibly to make — booklovers.

Brown University Library,
Commencement Day, 1916

TABLE OF CONTENTS

THE BOOKLOVER AND HIS BOOKS

THE BOOKLOVER AND HIS BOOKS

BOOKS AND BOOKLOVERS[1]

THE booklover is distinguished from the reader as such by loving his books, and from the collector as such by reading them. He prizes not only the soul of the book, but also its body, which he would make a house beautiful, meet for the indwelling of the spirit given by its author. Love is not too strong a word to apply to his regard, which demands, in the language of Dorothy Wordsworth, "a beautiful book, a book to caress—peculiar, distinctive, individual: a book that hath first caught your eye and then pleased your fancy." The truth is that the book on its physical side is a highly organized art object. Not in vain has it transmitted the thought and passion of the ages; it has taken toll of them, and in the hands of its worthiest makers these elements have worked themselves out into its material body. Enshrining the artist's thought, it has, therefore, the qualities of a true art product, and stands second only to those which express it, such as painting and sculpture; but no other art product of its own order, not the violin nor the jewel-casket, can compare with the book in esthetic quality. It

[1] The substance of an address delivered Nov. 18, 1909, in the Boston Public Library, under the auspices of the Society of Printers.

meets one of the highest tests of art, for it can appeal to the senses of both beauty and grandeur, either separately, as in the work of Aldus and of Sweynheym and Pannartz, or together, as in that of Jenson.

Books have doubtless had their lovers in all ages, under all their forms. Even the Assyrian clay tablet, if stamped with the words of poet or sage, might have shared the affection which they inspired. So might the papyrus roll of the Egyptian, and so does even to-day the parchment book of the middle ages, whenever its fortunate owner has the soul of a booklover. From this book our own was derived, yet not without a break. For our book is not so much a copy of the Roman and medieval book as a "substitute" for it, a machine product made originally to sell at a large profit for the price of hand-work. It was fortunate for the early printed book that it stood in this intimate if not honored relation to the work of the scribes and illuminators, and fortunate for the book of to-day, since, with all its lapses, it cannot escape its heritage of those high standards.

Mr. John Cotton Dana has analyzed the book into forty elements; a minuter analysis might increase the number to sixty; but of either number the most are subsidiary, a few controlling. The latter are those of which each, if decided upon first, determines the character of the rest; they include size, paper, and type. The mention of any size, folio, quarto, octavo, twelvemo, sixteenmo, calls up at once a distinct mental picture of an ideal book for each dimension, and the series is marked by a decreasing thickness of paper and size of type as it progresses downward from the folio. The proportions of the page will also vary, as well as the surface of the paper and the cut of the type, the other elements conforming to that first chosen.

Next to size, paper determines the expression of a book. It

is the printing material par excellence; but for its production the art could never have flourished. It is as much preferred by the printer as parchment was by the scribe. Its three elements of body, surface, and tint must all be considered, and either body or surface may determine the size of the book or the character of the type. A smooth surface may be an element of beauty, as with the paper employed by Baskerville, but it must not be a shiny surface. The great desideratum in modern paper from the point of view of the book-buyer is a paper that, while opaque and tough, shall be thin enough to give us our books in small compass, one more akin to the dainty and precious vellum than to the heavier and coarser parchment. It should also be durable.

Type gives its name to the art and is the instrument by which the spoken word is made visible to the eye. The aims in its design should be legibility, beauty, and compactness, in this order; but these are more or less conflicting qualities, and it is doubtful if any one design can surpass in all. Modern type is cleaner-cut than the old, but it may be questioned whether this is a real gain. William Morris held that all types should avoid hair-lines, fussiness, and ugliness. Legibility should have the right of way for most printed matter, especially children's books and newspapers. If the latter desire compactness, they should condense their style, not their types.

A further important element, which affects both the legibility and the durability of the book, is the ink. For most purposes it should be a rich black. Some of the print of the early masters is now brown, and there have been fashions of gray printing, but the booklover demands black ink, except in ornaments, and there color, if it is to win his favor, must be used sparingly and with great skill. We are told that the best combination for the eye is ink of a bluish tint on buff-tinted paper; but, like much other good advice, this remains practically untried.

Illustrations have been a feature of the book for over four hundred years, but they have hardly yet become naturalized within its pages. Or shall we say that they soon forgot their proper subordination to the type and have since kept up a more or less open revolt? The law of fitness demands that whatever is introduced into the book in connection with type shall harmonize with the relatively heavy lines of type. This the early black-line engravings did. But the results of all other processes, from copper-plate to half-tone, conflict with the type-picture and should be placed where they are not seen with it. Photogravures, for instance, may be put at the end of the book, or they may be covered with a piece of opaque tissue paper, so that either their page or the facing type-page will be seen alone. We cannot do without illustrations. All mankind love a picture as they love a lover. But let the pictures belong to the book and not merely be thrust into it.

The binding is to the book what the book is to its subject-matter, a clothing and protection. In the middle ages, when books were so few as to be a distinction, they were displayed sidewise, not edgewise, on the shelves, and their covers were often richly decorated, sometimes with costly gems. Even the wooden cover of the pre-Columbian Mexican book had gems set in its corners. Modern ornamentation is confined to tooling, blind and gilt, and inlaying. But some book-lovers question whether any decoration really adds to the beauty of the finest leather. It should be remembered that the binding is not all on the outside. The visible cover is only the jacket of the real cover on which the integrity of the book depends. The sewing is the first element in time and importance. To be well bound a book should lie open well, otherwise it is bound not for the reader but only for the collector.

It cannot be too often repeated that properly made books are not extremely costly. A modern book offered at a fancy price means either a very small edition, an extravagant binding, or what is more likely, a gullible public. But most books that appeal to the booklover are not excessive in price. Never before was so much money spent in making books attractive—for the publisher always has half an eye on the booklover—and while much of this money is wasted, not all is laid out in vain. Our age is producing its quota of good books, and these the booklover makes it his business to discover.

In order to appreciate, the booklover must first know. He must be a book-kenner, a critic, but one who is looking for excellencies rather than faults, and this knowledge there are many books to teach him. But there is no guide that can impart the love of books; he must learn to love them as one learns to love sunsets, mountains, and the ocean, by seeing them. So let him who would know the joys and rewards of the booklover associate with well-made books. Let him begin with the ancients of printing, the great Germans, Italians, Dutchmen. He can still buy their books if he is well-to-do, or see them in libraries and museums if he belongs to the majority. Working down to the moderns, he will find himself discriminating and rejecting, but he will be attracted by certain printers and certain periods in the last four hundred years, and he will be rejoiced to find that the last thirty years, though following a decline, hold their own —not by their mean but by their best—with any former period short of the great first half-century, 1450–1500.

Finally, if his book-love develops the missionary spirit in him, let him lend his support to the printers and publishers of to-day who are producing books worthy of the booklover's regard, for in no other way can he so effectually speed the day when all books shall justify the emotion which more than five hundred years ago Richard de Bury, Bishop of Durham, expressed in the title of his famous and still cherished work, the *Philobiblon*.

FITNESS IN BOOK DESIGN

A WOMAN'S fitness comes by fits," said slanderous Cloten; but to say as much of fitness in book design would be on the whole a compliment. Fitness as applied to book design means, of course, that the material form of the book shall correspond to its spiritual substance, shall be no finer and no meaner, and shall produce a like, even if a slighter, esthetic impression. At the outset we have to surrender to commercialism more than half our territory. All agree that our kings should be clothed in purple and our commoners in broadcloth; but how about the intellectual riffraff that makes up the majority of our books? Are our publishers willing that these should be clothed according to their station? Hardly; for then would much of their own occupation be gone. It is recognized that for a large proportion of our publications the design—the outward appearance—is in great measure counted on to sell the book; and printers and publishers will not consent to send the paupers of literature forth upon the world in their native rags, for so they would find no one to welcome them. It will be useless to quarrel with the fact that the design of many books is meant as a bait and not as a simple interpretation of their meaning and worth. Design of this character, however, is relatively easy; it is really not design at all, but millinery. It is when his work becomes genuinely interpretative that the designer's difficulties begin.

The first business of the designer, therefore, is to understand the book he is treating. Here, of course, his judgment, however sincere, may be mistaken or misled. A classical instance of this is found in connection with one of the most famous books in the history of modern printing,—Barlow's "Columbiad." This work, which first appeared in 1787 under a different title, was enlarged to epic proportions during the next twenty years, and was finally given to the world in 1807 in the belief on the part of its author and in the hope at least on the part of its publisher that it would take rank and be honored for all time as the great American epic. Under this misconception the book was clothed in a form that might worthily have enshrined "Paradise Lost." Its stately quarto pages were set in a type specially designed for the work and taking from it the name of Columbian. The volume was embellished with full-page engravings after paintings in the heroic manner by Smirke; in short, it was the most pretentious book issued in America up to that time, and it still ranks, in the words of Professor Barrett Wendell, "among the most impressive books to look at in the world." But alas for the vanity of human aspirations! "The Columbiad" is now remembered as a contribution to typography rather than literature. The designer overshot his author.

We have tacitly assumed that a book has but one interpretation and therefore but one most appropriate design. This, however, is far from the truth. When, after various more or less successful editions of Irving's "Knickerbocker" had appeared, Mr. Updike brought out some twenty years ago his comic edition, with the whole make-up of the book expressive of the clumsy and stupid Dutchmen depicted in Irving's mock-heroic, we felt at the moment that here was the one ideal "Knickerbocker." Yet, much as we still admire it, does it wholly satisfy us? Is there not as much room as ever for an edition that shall express primarily not the absurdity of its subject-matter, but the delicate playfulness of Irving's humor and the lightness and grace of his exuberant style? Has there ever been a final "Don Quixote"? Certainly not in the recent monumental editions with their quagmire of footnotes. Moreover, if *we* had a final edition of the great romance it would not remain final for our children's children. Every age will make its own interpretations of the classics and will demand that they be embodied in contemporary design. Thus every age in its book design mirrors itself for future admiration or contempt.

Obviously, in giving form to a single work a designer is freer than in handling a series by one or by various authors. In such cases he must seize upon more general and therefore less salient characteristics. The designer of "Hiawatha" or "Evangeline" has a fairly clear task before him, with a chance of distinct success or failure; but the designer of an appropriate form for the whole series of Longfellow's works, both prose and poetry, has a less individualized problem, and must think of the elements that run through all, — sweetness, grace, gentleness, dignity, learning. Yet, though general, these qualities in a series may be far from vague. We have only to consider the absurdity of a handy-volume Gibbon or a folio Lamb. On looking at the bulky, large-type, black-covered volumes of the Forman edition of Shelley and Keats one instinctively asks, "What crime did these poets commit that they should be so impounded?" The original edition of the life of Tennyson by his son, in two lumbering, royal octavo volumes, comes near to what Thackeray called the Farnese Hercules, "a hulking abortion." Contrast with it the dignity linked with charm of the original edition of Longfellow's life by his brother. But of all monstrosities of book design the British three-volume novel mania is responsible for some of the worst. Henry Ward Beecher's one novel, "Norwood," which appeared in America becomingly clad in a single volume, received in England the regulation three-volume dress, in which it looks as ridiculously inflated as did a slender miss of that period in the crinoline then in vogue. There is one abomination in book design for which I owe a personal grudge to commercialism, and that is the dropsical book form given to Locker-Lampson's "My Confidences." If ever there was a winsome bit of writing it is this, and it should have made a book to take to one's heart, something not larger than a "Golden Treasury" volume, but of individual design. My comfort is that this will yet be done, and my belief is that art will justify itself better in the market than commercialism did. A more modern instance of expansion for commercial reasons defeating fitness in design is furnished by Waters' translation of "The Journal of Montaigne's Travels." Here we have three small volumes outwardly attractive, but printed on paper thick enough for catalogue cards, and therefore too stiff for the binding, also in type too large to be pleasant. The whole should have been issued in one volume of the same size in smaller type, and would then have been as delightful in form as it is in substance.

It is not enough that all the elements of a book be honest, sincere, enduring; otherwise the clumsy royal octavos of Leslie Stephen's edition of Fielding would be as attractive as "the dear and dumpy twelves" of the original editions. Royal octavo, indeed, seems to be the pitfall of the book designer, though there is no inherent objection to it. Where in the whole range of reference books will be found a more attractive set of volumes than Moulton's "Library of Literary Criticism," with their realization in this format of the Horatian *simplex munditiis?* For extremely different treatments of this book size it is instructive to compare the slender volumes of the original editions of Ruskin with the slightly shorter but very much thicker volumes of the scholarly definitive edition, which is a monument of excellence in every element of book design except the crowning one of fitness. Our libraries must have this edition for its completeness and its editorship; its material excellence will insure the transmission of Ruskin's message to future centuries; but no one will ever fall in love with these volumes or think of likening them to the marriage of "perfect music unto noble words."

Granted that the designer knows the tools of his trade,—grasps the expressional value of every element with which he has to deal, from the cut of a type to the surface of a binder's cloth,—his task, as we said, is first to know the soul of the book intrusted to him for embodiment; it is next to decide upon its most characteristic quality, or the sum of its qualities; and, lastly, it is so to use his physical elements as to give to the completed book an expression that shall be the outward manifestation of its indwelling spirit. This is all that can be asked of him; but, if he would add a touch of perfection, let him convey the subtle tribute of a sense of the value of his subject by reflecting in his design the artist's joy in his work.

PRINT AS AN INTERPRETER OF MEANING

THE invention of printing, we have often been told, added to book production only the two commercial elements of speed and cheapness. As regards the book itself, we are assured, printing not only added nothing, but, during the four and a half centuries of its development, has constantly tended to take away. These statements are no doubt historically and theoretically true, yet they are so unjust to the present-day art that some supplementary statement of our obligations to printing seems called for, aside from the obvious rejoinder that, even if speed and cheapness are commercial qualities, they have reached a development—especially in the newspaper—beyond the dreams of the most imaginative fifteenth-century inventor, and have done nothing less than revolutionize the world.

Taking the service of printing as it stands to-day, what does it actually do for the reader? What is the great difference between the printed word and even the best handwriting? It is obviously the condensation and the absolute mechanical sameness of print. The advantage of these differences to the eye in respect to rapid reading is hardly to be overestimated. Let any one take a specimen of average penmanship and note the time which he consumes in reading it; let him compare with this the time occupied in reading the same number of printed words, and the difference will be startling; but not even so will it do justice to print, for handwriting average in quality is very far from average in frequency. If it be urged that the twentieth-century comparison should be between typewriting and print, we may reply that typewriting *is* print, though it lacks most of its condensation, and that the credit for its superior legibility belongs to typography, of which the new art is obviously a by-product. But we are not yet out of the manuscript period, so far as private records are concerned, and it still is true, as it has been for many generations, that print multiplies the years of every scholar's and reader's life.

At this point we may even introduce a claim for print as a contributor to literature. There are certainly many books of high literary standing that never would have attained their present form without the intervention of type. It is well known that Carlyle rewrote his books in proof, so that the printer, instead of attempting to correct his galleys, reset them outright. Balzac went a step further, and largely wrote his novels in proof, if such an expression may be allowed. He so altered and expanded them that what went to the printing office as copy for a novelette finally came out of it a full-sized novel. Even where the changes are not so extensive, as in the proof-sheets of the Waverley Novels preserved in the Cornell University Library, it is interesting to trace the alterations which the author was prompted to make by the sight of his paragraphs clothed in the startling distinctness of print. Nor is this at all surprising when one considers how much better the eye can take in the thought and style of a composition from the printed page than it can even from typewriting. The advantage is so marked that some publishers, before starting on an expensive literary venture, are accustomed to have the copy set up on the linotype for the benefit of their critics. If the work is accepted, the revisions are made on these sheets, and then, finally, the work is sent back to the composing room to receive the more elaborate typographic dress in which it is to appear.

But to return to the advantages of type to the reader. Handwriting can make distinctions, such as punctuation and paragraphing, but print can greatly enforce them. The meaning of no written page leaps out to the eye; but this is the regular experience of the reader with every well-printed page. While printing can do nothing on a single page that is beyond the power of a skillful penman, its ordinary resources are the extraordinary ones of manuscript. It might not be physically impossible, for instance, to duplicate with a pen a page of the Century Dictionary, but it would be practically impossible, and, if the pen were our only resource, we never should have such a marvel of condensation and distinctness as that triumph of typography in the service of scholarship.

In ordinary text, printing has grown away from the distinctions to the eye that were in vogue two hundred years ago—a gain to art and perhaps to legibility also, though contemporary critics like Franklin lamented the change—but in reference books we have attained to a finer skill in making distinctions to the eye than our forefathers achieved with all their typographic struggles. Nor are our reference pages lacking in beauty. But our familiarity with works of this class tends to obscure their wonderful merit as time-savers and eye-savers. It is only when we take up some foreign dictionary, printed with little contrast of type, perhaps in German text, and bristling with unmeaning abbreviations, that we appreciate our privilege. Surely this is a marvelous mechanical triumph, to present the words of an author in such a form that the eye, to take it in, needs but to sweep rapidly down the page, or, if it merely glances at the page, it shall have the meaning of the whole so focused in a few leading words that it can turn at once to the passage sought, or see that it must look elsewhere. The saving of time so effected may be interpreted either as a lengthening of life or as an increased fullness of life, but it means also a lessening of friction and thus an addition to human comfort.

We have been speaking of prose; but print has done as much or more to interpret the meaning of poetry. We have before us a facsimile of nineteen lines from the oldest Vatican manuscript of Vergil. The hexameters are written in single lines; but this is the only help to the eye. The letters are capitals and are individually very beautiful, indeed, the lines are like ribbons of rich decoration; but the words are not separated, and the punctuation is inconspicuous and primitively simple, consisting merely of faint dots. Modern poetry, especially lyric, with its wealth and interplay of rhyme, affords a fine opportunity for the printer to mediate between the poet and his public, and this he has been able to do by mere indention and leading, without resorting to distinction of type. The reader of a sonnet or ballad printed without these two aids to the eye is robbed of his rightful clues to the construction of the verse. It seems hardly possible that a poem could have been read aloud from an ancient manuscript, at sight, with proper inflection; yet this is just what printing can make possible for the modern reader. It has not usually done so, for the printer has been very conservative; he has taken his conception of a page from prose, and, not being compelled to, has not placed all the resources of his art at the service of the poet. Accents, pauses, and certain arbitrary signs might well be employed to indicate to the reader the way the poet meant his line to be read. Milton curiously gave us some metric hints by means of changes in spelling, but we have to read all our other poets in the light of our own discernment, and it is not to be wondered at if doctors disagree. Even the caesura, or pause in the course of a long line, is not always easy to place. Francis Thompson, in his poem "A Judgement in Heaven," has indicated this by an asterisk, giving an example that might well be followed by other poets and their printers. The regularity of eighteenth-century verse made little call for guide-posts, but modern free meter, in proportion to its greater flexibility and richness, demands more assistance to the reader's eye, or even to his understanding. For instance, to read aloud hexameters or other long lines, some of which have the initial accent on the first syllable and some later, is quite impossible without previous study supplemented by a marking of the page. Yet a few printed accents would make a false start impossible. Poetry will never require the elaborate aid from the printer which he gives to music; but it seems clear that he has not yet done for it all that he might or should.

It is surely not an extreme assumption that the first duty of the printer is to the meaning of his author, and his second to esthetics; but shall we not rather say that his duty is to meet both demands, not by a compromise, but by a complete satisfaction of each? A difficult requirement, surely, but one that we are confident the twentieth-century printer will not permit his critics to pronounce impossible.

FAVORITE BOOK SIZES

IN the following paper some account will be given of five book sizes that have taken rank as favorites. It should excite no surprise that all are small sizes. Nature's favorites are always small; her insect jewels outnumber her vertebrates a millionfold; and book-loving human nature takes the same delight in daintiness.

There is, to be sure, a general impression that the first centuries of printing were given up to folios, the eighteenth century to quartos and octavos, and that only the present period has been characterized by twelvemos and sixteenmos. We think of the Gutenberg Bible, the Nuremberg Chronicle, the mighty editions of the Fathers, the polyglot Bibles of Paris, London, and Antwerp, — fairly to be called limp teachers' Bibles, — the 1611 Bible, the Shakespeare folios; then of the quarto editions of Addison, Pope, Walpole, and their contemporaries, and the stately octavo editions of the same writers; and finally of the myriad *infra* that have swarmed from the press during the last century. But, when we walk through a library that offers a representative collection of books from the invention of printing to the present, we realize that the bigness of the folios and quartos has deceived us as to their relative number, all forms of literature being considered.

The parent of our present book form, the Roman codex, split from an actual block of wood, had a surface hardly as large as the cover of a Little Classic. The vellum Books of Hours were dainty volumes. Even in the period between Gutenberg and Aldus, books of moderate size were not uncommon, and continuously, from the days of the great Venetian popularizer of literature to the present, the small books have far outnumbered their heavy-armed allies. Common sense, indeed, would tell us that this must be so, even if it had not inspired Dr. Johnson, its eighteenth century exponent, to declare: "Books that you may carry to the fire, and hold readily in your hand, are the most useful after all."

Our account properly begins with Aldus. From 1494, the date of his first productions, until 1501 he printed his books in folio and quarto. But in the first year of the new century he began to use his famous cursive type, now called italic. The fineness of the new type, as has been suggested, called for a smaller size of book, which was also favored by considerations of economy and convenience; and so Aldus made up his sheets in a form which the fold compels us to call octavo, but which to-day would be called sixteenmo. Says Horatio F. Brown, in his "The Venetian Printing Press": "The public welcomed the new type and size. The College granted Aldus a monopoly for ten years for all books printed in this manner. The price of books was lowered at once. Didot calculates that an octavo of Aldus cost, on an average, two francs and a half, whereas a folio probably cost about twenty francs. These two innovations on type and on format constituted a veritable revolution in the printing press and in the book trade, which now began to reach a far more extensive market than it had ever touched before. With this wide diffusion of books came the popularization of knowledge at which Aldus aimed. Scholarship began to lose its exclusive and aristocratic character when the classics were placed within the reach of any student who chose to study, meditate, and interpret them for himself. And to Aldus belongs the credit of having, through his new type and size, opened the way to the democratization of learning."

That the taste which Aldus so successfully hit was no merely temporary one, any person will be convinced if he will stand before a shelf full of these little Aldus classics, handle the light, well-proportioned volumes, and take in the esthetic charm of their type and page and form, which, in spite of their four hundred years, by no means savors of antiquity. In these books Aldus achieved one of the greatest triumphs possible in any art, a union of beauty and utility, each on so high a plane that no one is able to decide which is pre-eminent. In a copy which I have before me of his "Rhetoricorum ad C. Herennium Libri IIII," 1546, the fine proportions of the page appear in spite of trimming. Very noticeable are the undersized roman capitals; more curious is the letter printed in the otherwise blank square to indicate what initial the illuminator should insert in color, and the irregular use of capitals and small letters after a period. The catchword appears only on the last page of the signature, not on every page, as was the later practice. Modern usage wisely consigns italic to a subordinate place, but in point of beauty combined with convenience, it may well be questioned if four centuries of printing have made any advance upon this page.

In nearly every library for scholars is to be found a row of plump little books that never fail to catch the eye of the sightseer. If the visitor does not know beforehand what they are, he is little enlightened on being told that they are "Elzevirs," and the attendant must needs supply the information that the Elzevirs were a family of Dutch printers who flourished during the century that closed with the arrival of

William III in England, and that these tiny volumes represent their most popular productions. Says George Haven Putnam in his "Books and their Makers during the Middle Ages": "The Elzevirs, following the example set a century and a half earlier by Aldus, but since that time very generally lost sight of by the later publishers, initiated a number of series of books in small and convenient forms, twelvemo and sixteenmo, which were offered to book buyers at prices considerably lower than those they had been in the habit of paying for similar material printed in folio, quarto, or octavo. . . . These well-edited, carefully printed, and low-priced editions of the classics won for the Elzevirs the cordial appreciation of scholars and of students throughout Europe."

Among the authors who acknowledged their indebtedness to the Elzevirs may be mentioned Galileo, the elder Balzac, and the poet Ménage. I have before me more than six feet of shelving filled with these tiny books. They are nearly all bound in vellum, and thus retain their antique appearance without as well as within. Their subject-matter is in the fields of literature, ancient and contemporary, and the history, geography, and political constitution of the principal countries. The books of the latter division are known as "Respublicæ Variæ." It is impossible to resist the conclusion that this book form was chosen not more to supply cheap books which could be sold to impecunious scholars than to provide portable volumes for travelers. The Elzevir "Commonwealths" were the predecessors of our "satchel guides," and the literary publications in this form were evidently designed to be pocket editions. It was to such books that Dr. Johnson referred when he advised his friends "never to go out without some little book or other in their pocket. Much time is lost by waiting, by travelling, etc., and this may be prevented by making use of every possible opportunity for improvement." When the positive doctor, on his journey to the Hebrides, paid his tribute to George Buchanan at St. Andrews, his acquaintance with the Latin poetry of the Scotch professor may well have arisen from his having thus made a pocket piece of one of the several Elzevir editions of the poet.

The characteristics of the "Elzevirs" are that they range from about four to about five inches in height, are always narrow, 2¼ to 2¾ inches in width, and are usually thick, in some cases even 1½ inches. It is hardly necessary to say that the esthetic impression of these "jewels of typography" is wholly different from that produced by the "Alduses." It is the beauty of an infant compared with that of a youth, and, as in the case of the infant, plumpness is a part of the charm. The thinnest of the "Elzevirs" (about three-fourths of an inch thick) lack much of the characteristic quality. It is of course granted that no small portion of the charm exerted by these volumes is due to their type, which in artistic excellence and practical effectiveness has hardly been surpassed before or since.

When William Pickering, in 1830, began to issue his Aldine edition of the British Poets in the most beautiful and appropriate form that he could devise, the design which he placed upon the title-page, a dolphin and an anchor, with the words "Aldi discip. Anglus," was an expression at once of pride and of obligation. He had gone back to Aldus for his model, and the book which he produced was in all but its change of type from italic to roman a nearly exact reproduction of the form which Aldus had employed so successfully three centuries before. Even the relative thinness of the volumes was preserved as an important element of their attractiveness to eye and hand. Whoever would learn what an enormous difference in esthetic effect can be produced by slight differences in style and size, especially in thickness, should compare the Pickering "Aldines" with the rival set of British Poets published by Little and Brown. The latter series is a noble one, often showing better presswork than Pickering's, and it was deservedly popular, but it is many degrees removed from the totality of esthetic charm that would entitle it to rank as a favorite.

We said that Pickering went back to Aldus for his model, but he did not travel a lonely road. The book size in question had never ceased to be used, and in the eighteenth century it was in full favor. The writings of the novelists and essayists found ready buyers in this form, as witness, among others, the Strahan Fielding of 1783, the Rivington Idler of the same year, and the Rivington Sterne of 1788. The size of the printed page is usually larger, but that of the Sterne corresponds as closely to that of the two "Aldines" as the difference in the size of type will permit. Pickering's contemporaries and successors in the publishing field recognized the attractiveness of this book size, and the works of the poets generally were issued in this form; hence we have, for example, the Longman Southey, the Moxon Wordsworth, and the Murray Crabbe. The latest series to appeal for popular favor by the use of this book form is Everyman's Library, in which, though much has been sacrificed to cheapness, the outward proportions of the volumes are almost identical with those adopted by Aldus and Pickering.

> Go, little book, whose pages hold
>   Those garnered years in loving trust;
> How long before your blue and gold
>   Shall fade and whiten in the dust?

This stanza from Dr. Holmes's introduction to his "Poems" of 1862 may well be claimed by the Blue and Gold edition of the poets as its passport to the recognition of future generations. But it will need no passport; its own enduring charm is sufficient. The volumes of this dainty series, while larger in all but thickness than the "Elzevirs," yet make their appeal by much the same qualities, compactness and portability, with a suggestion of the Elzevirian plumpness. To the attraction of the size is added the contrasted charm of the blue cover and the gilt stamp and edges. That a Blue and Gold edition, in the absence of its name qualities, becomes something far inferior may be seen from a copy that has lost them in rebinding. In spite of the hardness of their blue and the crudeness of their stamped designs, these little volumes attract every reader and never remain long on the shelves of the second-hand bookstores. We should not expect a publisher to succeed were he now to put them upon the market for the first time or in an exact reproduction. But the publisher who shall so recombine their elements as to produce upon his public the effect which they made upon theirs, and which they still make as reminiscent of an earlier taste, will be the envy of his fellows. It is interesting to note that after fifty years these volumes show no sign of fading, so that Dr. Holmes might well have made his stanza an exclamation instead of a question. They seem likely to last as long as the "Elzevirs" or even the "Alduses" have already lasted, and possibly to outlast the fame, though hardly the memory, of the poet who sang them. The dimensions of the cover are $5\frac{5}{8}$ by $3\frac{5}{8}$ inches; the thickness is about an inch. There was a larger Blue and Gold format, as well as several smaller, but only the standard is now valued.

We cannot bring our list of favorite book sizes much nearer the present without running the risk of confusing the temporary and the permanent in popular approval. We will, therefore, close with a mention of the Little Classics. At about the time when the Blue and Gold series ceased to be published, more exactly in 1874, Mr. Rossiter Johnson designed for the now famous series which he was then editing a book form that sprang at once into a favor that it still retains. In this form, which appears to have no near counterpart in either earlier or later bookmaking, the volumes are closely six by four inches by three-quarters of an inch in thickness. The edges are colored red, whatever the color of the sides. The printed page is relatively wide, and the whole effect of the book is that of a tiny quarto, though in reality the dimensions are those of a rather small sixteenmo of normal proportions. Thus the volume produces upon the eye the charm of daintiness, while the page contains a sufficient amount of matter to make the volume profitable to the purchaser.

This series naturally suggests comparison with the Tauchnitz editions, which consist of volumes only slightly larger. But really no comparison is possible. The Tauchnitz editions are merely convenient carriers of letterpress. The Little Classics are a genuine art product. That the latter book size has not been more widely used than it has, by its own and by other publishers, is perhaps due to commercial reasons. But there can be no question of the esthetic appeal which it makes upon the reader who is looking for compactness and beauty rather than for the greatest bulk for his money. With the modern demand for the saving of space in private libraries we may reasonably look for a revival of this condensed and charming book size.

The adoption of a few standard sizes for all books was urged some years ago at a meeting of American librarians. Commenting on this proposal, a New York publisher remarked that he should be glad to have such standard sizes adopted by others, but he should take pains to avoid them in his own publications in order to gain the distinction of difference. The discussion stopped suddenly under the impact of this unexpected assault. But a second thought shows that the publisher's comment leaves the question still open. It is obvious that if we were to adopt standard sizes based upon nothing more fundamental than the librarian's desire for uniformity or the printer's mechanical convenience, without regard to the tastes and preferences of the reader, who is the final judge, the publisher might well find his gain in disregarding them. But if the standards adopted all represented sizes long tested and approved by popular favor, the publisher who should avoid them would display a confidence in the Spirit of the Perverse as sublime as it would be hazardous. Fortunately no formal standardization of book sizes is likely to be attempted. But, keenly as a publisher would resent any limitation upon his freedom in book design, he is just as keenly desirous that his books shall be favorites. To attain his coveted end he has two resources, experience and experiment, or a mixture of both. While the book sizes that have been discussed in this chapter do not include all the favorites, they certainly include some of the first favorites, and are worthy of study by everyone who is seeking public favor in the design of that complex art product known as a Book.

THE VALUE OF READING, TO THE PUBLIC AND TO THE INDIVIDUAL

OF what value is it to a community to contain—still more to be composed of—well-read people? We can best answer this question by picturing its opposite, a community without readers; this we are unfortunately able to do without drawing upon our imaginations, for we have only to turn to certain districts of countries like Spain or Russia. There we shall meet whole communities, large enough to form cities elsewhere, which are little more than aggregations of paupers. Shall we find in any of these homes a daily or a weekly paper, or a monthly magazine, or even a stray book? Not one, except perhaps in the house of a priest. These masses of people live on the earth, to be sure, but they do not live in the world. No currents of the great, splendid life of the twentieth century ever reach them; and they live in equal isolation from the life of the past. "The glory that was Greece and the grandeur that was Rome" have for them simply no existence. They are truly the disinherited of all the ages. Though they may not be unhappy, they can be called nothing less than wretched. Is the fault one of race, or government, or religion? Much could be said on all these points, both for and against; but one fact remains indisputable—these people do not read.

Let us turn now to a different type of community, that represented by the ordinary New England village. How stands the cause of reading there? If there is any person of sound mind in the community who has never learned to read, he is pointed out as a curiosity. There is not a home in the length and breadth of the town that is without its paper, its magazine, or its books. In other words, literacy is taken for granted. Is it any wonder that in progress, wealth, and influence the one community starts where the other leaves off? In the illiterate towns just described there is often no man who has the slightest capacity for business or who can represent the interests of his community before even the humblest government official. But from towns of the other type come men who represent with honor their state and their nation; men who widen the bounds of freedom and who add new stars to the celestial sphere of knowledge. Is all this wholly a matter of reading? One would not dare to assert it absolutely, remembering the advantages of race, government, and religion enjoyed in New England. And yet we have only to fancy the condition of even such a town after one generation, supposing all its printed matter and its power to read were taken away, if we would realize what an impulse to progress and prosperity is given by the presence of the volumes that line the shelves of our public libraries.

If the fortunes of a community in the modern world are bound up with the use that it makes of books and libraries, no less are those of the individual. This is true whether we refer to his private satisfaction or to his public advancement. The animal is endowed with instinct, which is sufficient for the guidance of his life, but it permits of no development. Man must depend upon judgment, experience, reason — guides that are often only too blind; but at least they admit of progress. In fact it is only in the field of knowledge that human progress appears to be possible. We have no better bodies than the ancient Greeks had—to put the case very mildly. We have no better minds than they had—to make an even safer assertion. But we *know* almost infinitely more than they did. In this respect the ancient Greeks were but as children compared with ourselves. What makes this tremendous difference? Simply the fact that we know all that was known by them and the Romans and the men of the middle ages, and through this knowledge we have learned more by our own discovery than they knew, all put together. The path to success for men and races lies through the storehouse where this vast knowledge is garnered—the library. But it is something more than a storehouse of knowledge; it is an electrical battery of power. This knowledge, this power, can be obtained in its fullness only through books. The man, therefore, who aspires to lead his fellows, to command their respect or their votes, must not rely on native talent alone; he must add to it the stored-up talent of the ages.

There is an old proverb: "No man ever got rich with his coat off." This is a puzzling assertion, for it seems to contradict so many accepted ideas. General Grant, for instance, when asked for his coat-of-arms, replied: "A pair of shirt sleeves." The answer showed an honorable pride in labor; but we must remember that it was not General Grant's arms but his brain that won his victories. Does not our proverb mean simply this: that the great prizes of life—of which riches is the symbol, not the sum—cannot be won by main strength and ignorance; that they can be won only by energy making use of knowledge? But it is not only in the public successes of life that books have a value for the individual. Public successes are never the greatest that men win. It is in the expansion and uplift of the inner self that books render their grandest service. Emily Dickinson wrote of such a reader:

THE VALUE OF READING

He ate and drank the precious words,
  His spirit grew robust;
He knew no more that he was poor,
  Nor that his frame was dust.
He danced along the dingy days,
  And this bequest of wings
Was but a book What liberty
  A loosened spirit brings!

A final word on values. The philosophers make two great classes of values, which may be entitled respectively Property and Possessions. Under Property come money, houses, lands, carriages, clothing, jewels; under Possessions come love, friendship, morality, knowledge, culture, refinement. All are good things. There never were any houses or carriages or clothes too good for a human being. But these obviously belong to a different type of values from the other group—to a lower type. What is the test, the touchstone, by which we can tell to which class any value belongs? We shall find the test clearly stated in the Sermon on the Mount. Is the treasure in question one that moth and rust can corrupt or that thieves can break through and steal? If so, it belongs to the lower class, to Property. But if it is one that cannot be taken away, then it is a Possession and belongs to the higher type. There is another test, which is really a part of this: Can you share it without loss? If I own a farm, and give to another a half of it or a year's crop from it, I deprive myself of just so much. But, if I have knowledge or taste or judgment or affection, I can pour them all out like water for the benefit of my fellows, and yet never have any the less. On the contrary, I shall find that I have more; for they grow by sharing. But we have not yet done with the superiority of Possessions over Property. "Shrouds have no pockets," says the grim old proverb; and all Property must be laid down at the edge of the grave. But if man be immortal, as the wise in all ages have believed, then we do not have to lay down our Possessions with this mortal body. For, if the soul when freed from the flesh is to remain the soul, the self—and only so can immortality have any meaning—then it must keep all those inner acquisitions of knowledge, culture, and character which it has gathered on earth; nay, it then for the first time truly comes into the enjoyment of them. What were our earthly Possessions become Treasures laid up for ourselves in Heaven.

THE BOOK OF TO-DAY AND THE BOOK OF TO-MORROW

THE book of to-day is not necessarily the parent of the book of to-morrow, just as it is itself not necessarily the child of the book of yesterday. The relation is apt to be one of succession and influence rather than anything suggesting biological evolution. Nature, according to Linnaeus's famous maxim, never goes by leaps, but the book is a human product, and human nature takes its chief pride in its leaps, calling them inventions and discoveries. Such a leap in book production was the substitution of parchment for papyrus, of paper for parchment, of mechanical for manual processes when writing was displaced by typography, of higher for lower mechanism in the creation of the power perfecting press. These inventions had behind them, to be sure, the impetus of economic demand, but no such partial explanation can be given for the advent of William Morris among the printers of the late nineteenth century, unless an unrecognized artistic need may be said to constitute an economic demand.

The book of to-day in its best examples resembles not so much the book of yesterday as that of some earlier days, and we may count this fact a fortunate one, since it relegates to oblivion the books made in certain inartistic periods, notably of the one preceding the present revival. It is rather the best of the whole past of the book, and not the book of to-day alone, that influences the character to be taken by the book of to-morrow. This element is a historical one and a knowledge of it may be acquired by study; it is the possible inventions that baffle our prophecies. We know that any time some new process may be discovered that will transform the book into something as unlike its present character as that is unlike the papyrus roll. But because the element of invention is so uncertain we can only recognize it, we cannot take it into account. Our advantage in considering the book of to-day in connection with the book of to-morrow will be chiefly a negative one, in making the book as it is, so far as we find it defective, our point of departure in seeking the book as it ought to be.

To-day, for our present purposes, may be taken as beginning with the great work of Morris. But its book includes the worst as well as the best. It is not only the book by which we in our jealousy for the reputation of our age should like to have our age remembered, but also the more frequent book that we have to see and handle, however much against our will, and sometimes even to buy. We may congratulate ourselves that this book will perish by its own defects, leaving after all only the best book to be associated with our age; but this does not alter the fact that in the present the undesirable book is too much with us, is vastly in the majority, is, in fact, the only book that the great mass of our contemporaries know. How bad it is most book buyers do not realize; if they did, a better book would speedily take its place. But, until they do, our only chance of relief is the doubtful one of an invention that shall make good books cheaper to make than poor ones, or the difficult one of educating the public in the knowledge of what a book should be. The latter is obviously our only rational hope; but before we turn to consider it, let us first look at the book of to-day to see exactly what it is.

THE BOOK OF TO-DAY AND TO-MORROW

The book of to-day is first of all a novel. It has other forms, to be sure,—poetry, essays, history, travels, works of science and art,—but these do not meet the eye of the multitude. We may disregard them for the moment, and, in reply to the question, What is the book of to-day? we may say: It is a one-volume novel, a rather clumsy duodecimo, with a showy cover adorned with a colored picture of the heroine. It is printed on thick paper of poor quality, with type too large for the page, and ugly margins equal all around. Its binding is weak, often good for only a dozen readings, though quite as lasting as the paper deserves. For merits it can usually offer clear type, black ink, and good presswork. But its great fault is that in addressing the buyer it appeals to the primitive instinct for bigness rather than to the higher sense that regards quality. Such is the book of to-day, emphatically what Franklin over a hundred years ago called a "blown" book.

But though the novel fills the multitude's field of vision, it is after all not the only contemporary book; there are others from which we may be able to choose one worthier to be the book of to-day than the self-elected novel. But we shall not find it where commercialism is rife. In the presence of that element we find still only an appeal to the many—which, if successful, means large profits—by an appearance of giving much while really giving little. In this game of illusion the sound principles of bookmaking are forsaken. Books are not designed on the basis of what they are, but on the basis of what they can be made to seem. The result is puffery, not merely in advertising, but still earlier in the dimensions of the book itself—the most modern and profitable instance of using the east wind for a filler.

But at this point a new element is introduced, the public

library. The ordinary buyer carries home the distended book, and after he and his family have read it, he cares not if it falls to pieces after the next reading. Neither does he care if it takes up thrice the room that it should, for he no longer gives it room. But the public library, under the existing inflationism, must not only pay too much for its popular books; it must also house them at a needless outlay, and must very early duplicate a serious percentage of their first cost in rebinding them. So burdensome has this last item become that our libraries are consenting to pay a slightly larger first cost in order to avoid the necessity of rebinding; and enterprising publishers, following the lead of a more enterprising bookbinder, are beginning to cater to this library demand, which some day, let us hope, may dominate the entire publishing world for all books worth preserving, and may extend to all the elements of the book.

But fortunately there is here and there the uncommercial publisher and now and then an uncommercial mood in the ordinary publisher. To these we owe a small but important body of work of which no previous age need have been ashamed. Of these books we may almost say that they would be books if there were nothing in them. They have come into being by a happy conjunction of qualified publisher and appreciative buyers. They show what most books may be and what all books will strive to be if ever the majority of book buyers come to know what a good book is. This brings us finally to the book of to-morrow, what we hope it will be and how we can make it so.

The book of to-morrow, the book as it ought to be, will be both better and cheaper than the book of to-day. It can afford to be cheaper, for it will have a large and appreciative public, and for the same reason it will have to be better. The question of supreme importance now, if this public is ever to exist, is: How to educate our book buyers. The answer is not easy, for our book buyers do not realize that they are untrained, and, even if they realized it, the task of training them in the knowledge and love of the well-made book would be difficult. But we can do at least three things: agitate—proclaim the existence of a lore to be acquired, an ignorance and its practices to be eschewed; illustrate—show the good book and the bad together, and set forth, point by point, why the good is superior; last and most important, we must vindicate—back up our words by our deeds, support the publisher who gives the world good books, and leave to starvation or reform the publisher who clings to the old unworthy methods of incapacity or fraud. Even now, if every enlightened booklover in America would carry out this plan as a matter of duty merely where he could do so without inconvenience, nothing less than a revolution would be upon us, and we should have the Book of To-morrow while it is still To-day.

A CONSTRUCTIVE CRITIC OF THE BOOK

AT the meeting of the British librarians at Cambridge in 1882 a bomb was thrown into the camp of the book producers in the form of the question: Who spoils our new English books? In the explosion which followed, everybody within range was hit, from "the uncritical consumer" to "the untrained manufacturer." This dangerous question was asked and answered by Henry Stevens of Vermont, who, as a London bookseller, had for nearly forty years handled the products of the press new and old, had numbered among his patrons such critical booklovers as John Carter Brown and James Lenox, and had been honored with the personal friendship of William Pickering the publisher and Charles Whittingham the printer. He had therefore enjoyed abundant opportunity for qualifying himself to know whereof he spoke. If his words were severe, he stood ready to justify them with an exhibit of sixty contemporary books which he set before his hearers.[1]

The truth is, however unwilling his victims may have been to admit it, that his attack was only too well timed. The men of creative power, who had ennobled English book production during the second quarter of the nineteenth cen-

[1] The address here summarized was printed at the Chiswick Press and published at Christmas, 1884. Mr. Stevens died early in 1886, leaving a posthumous book entitled "Recollections of Mr. James Lenox," which was printed in the same year at the Chiswick Press, and which is of great interest to booklovers, especially Americans.

tury, had passed away, and books were being thrown together instead of being designed as formerly. The tradition of excellence in English bookmaking still held sway over the public, and, as their books sold, most producers saw no reason to disturb themselves. What to them was progress in other lands, or the claims of a future that could not be enforced? But after Mr. Stevens's attack they could at least no longer plead ignorance of their faults. It is certain that an improvement soon began, which culminated in the present great era of book design throughout the English world. If the famous bookseller's address were not the cause of the change, it at least marked a turning point, and it deserves to be studied as one of the historic documents of modern printing. It is more than this, however; it is a piece of creative criticism, and though teaching not by example but by contraries, it forms one of the best existing brief compends of what a well-made book must be.

The critic of books as they were made a generation ago begins with the assertion of a truth that cannot be too often repeated: "The manufacture of a beautiful and durable book costs little if anything more than that of a clumsy and unsightly one." He adds that once a handsome book and a new English book were synonymous terms, but that now the production of really fine books is becoming one of England's lost arts. He indulges in a fling at "the efforts of certain recent printers to retrieve this decadence by throwing on to the already overburdened trade several big, heavy, and voluminous works of standard authors termed 'éditions de luxe.'" He assures his hearers that his judgments were not formed on the spur of the moment, but were based partly on long personal observations—Stevens was the author of that widely influential piece of selective bibliography, "My English Library," London, 1853—and on the results of the international exhibitions since 1851, especially those of Vienna (1874), Philadelphia (1876), and Paris (1878), in the last of which he was a juror. His conclusion is "that the present new English, Scotch, and Irish books, of a given size and price, are not of the average quality of high art and skill in manufacture that is found in some other countries." He reminds his hearers that "it is no excuse to say that the rapidity of production has been largely increased. That amounts merely to confessing that we are now consuming two bad books in the place of one good one."

Mr. Stevens now comes to the direct question: Who spoils our new English books? He answers it by naming not less than ten parties concerned: (1) the author, (2) the publisher, (3) the printer, (4) the reader, (5) the compositor, (6) the pressman or machinist, (7) the papermaker, (8) the ink maker, (9) the bookbinder, and (10), last but not least, the consumer. There is no question of honesty or dishonesty, he says, but there is a painful lack of harmony, the bungling work of one or the clumsy manipulation of another often defeating the combined excellence of all the rest. The cure he foresees in the establishment of a school of typography, in which every disciple of these ten tribes shall study a recognized grammar of book manufacture based on the authority of the best examples.

He now returns to the charge and pays his respects to each member of the "ten tribes" in turn. The author's offense is found to consist largely of ignorant meddling. The publisher is too often ignorant, fussy, unskilled, pedantic, shiftless, and money-seeking, willing to make books unsightly if their cheapness will sell them. The printer is the scapegoat, and many books are spoiled in spite of his efforts, while he gets all the blame. But he is apt to have faults of his own, the worst of which is a failure in the careful design of the books intrusted to him. "It was not so," says Mr. Stevens, "with our good old friends William Pickering and Charles Whittingham, publisher and printer, working for many years harmoniously together. It was their custom, as both used repeatedly to tell us, to each first sit upon every new book and painfully hammer out in his own mind its ideal form and proportions. Then two Sundays at least were required to compare notes in the little summer house in Mr. Whittingham's garden at Chiswick, or in the after-dinner sanctuary, to settle the shape and dress of their forthcoming 'friend of man.' It was amusing as well as instructive to see each of them, when they met, pull from his bulging side pocket well-worn title-pages and sample leaves for discussion and consideration. When they agreed, perfection was at hand, and the 'copy' went forward to the compositors, but not till then. The results, to this day, are seen in all the books bearing the imprint of William Pickering, nearly all of which bear also evidence that they came from the 'Chiswick Press.'"

The reader, Mr. Stevens holds to be, under the printer, the real man of responsibility; but he too is often hampered by want of plan and due knowledge of the proportions of the book that he is handling. He also should go to the school of typography, and the readers of different offices should learn to agree. The compositor is pronounced "a little person of great consequence." His moral responsibility is not great, but too much is often thrust upon him; in fact he is, in many cases, the real maker of the book. "He ought to have a chance at the school of typography, and be better instructed in his own business, and be taught not to assume the business of any other sinner joined with him in the manufacture of books." Between the compositor and the pressman is a long road in which many a book is spoiled, but the responsibility is hard to place. Few people have any idea what constitute the essentials of a book's form and proportions. Yet our old standards, in manuscript and print, demand "that the length of a printed page should have relation to its width, and that the top should not exceed half the bottom margin, and that the front should be double the back margin."

The papermaker comes in for a large share of blame, but the remedy lies only in the hands of the consumer, who must insist on receiving good and durable paper. "The inkmaker is a sinner of the first magnitude." The first printing inks are still bright, clean, and beautiful after four hundred years; but who will give any such warrant to even the best inks of the present day? Mr. Stevens pronounces the sallow inks of our day as offensive to sight as they are to smell. The bookbinder is adjudged equal in mischief to any other of the ten sinners, and the rest are called upon to combine to prevent their books from being spoiled in these last hands.

The consumer, after all, is the person most to blame, for he has the power to control all the rest. Or, in the critic's closing words: "Many of our new books are unnecessarily spoiled, and it matters little whether this or that fault be laid to this or that sinner. The publisher, the printer, or the binder may sometimes, nay, often does, if he can, shift the burden of his sins to the shoulders of his neighbor, but all the faults finally will come back on the consumer if he tolerates this adulteration longer."

The great constructive feature of Mr. Stevens's address, which is one that brings it absolutely up to date, is his call for a school of typography, which shall teach a recognized grammar of book manufacture, especially printing, a grammar as standard as Lindley Murray's. He believes that the art of bookmaking cannot be held to the practice of the laws of proportion, taste, and workmanship, which were settled once for all in the age of the scribes and the first printers, without the existence and pressure of some recognized authority. Such an authority, he holds, would be furnished by a school of typography. This, as we interpret it, would be not necessarily a school for journeymen, but a school for those who are to assume the responsibility too often thrown upon the journeymen, the masters of book production. With a large annual output of books taken up by a public none too deeply versed in the constituents of a well-made book, there would seem to be much hope for printing as an art from the existence of such an institution, which would be critical in the interest of sound construction, and one might well wish that the course in printing recently established at Harvard might at some time be associated with the name of its prophet of a generation ago, Henry Stevens of Vermont.

BOOKS AS A LIBRARIAN WOULD LIKE THEM

THE librarian is in a position more than any one else to know the disabilities of books. The author is interested in his fame and his emoluments, the publisher in his reputation and his profits. To each of these parties the sales are the chief test. But the librarian's interest in the book begins after the sale, and it continues through the entire course of the book's natural life. His interest, moreover, is all-round; he is concerned with the book's excellence in all respects, intellectual, esthetic, and physical. He is the one who has to live with it, literally to keep house with it; and his reputation is in a way involved with its character. He may, therefore, be allowed for once to have his say as to how he would like to have books made.

If a book is worth writing at all, it is worth writing three times: first to put down the author's ideas, secondly to condense their expression into the smallest possible compass, and thirdly so to arrange them that they shall be most easily taken into the mind, putting them not necessarily into logical order, but into psychological order. If the author will do this and can add the touch of genius, or—shall we say?—can suffuse his work with the quality of genius, then he has made an addition to literature. That, among all the books which the librarian has to care for, he finds so few that he can call additions to literature is one of his grievances. The three processes may, indeed, by a practiced hand be performed as one. The librarian is only anxious that they be performed and that he have the benefit.

With the publisher the librarian feels that he can speak still more bluntly than with the author, for it is against the publisher that the librarian cherishes one of his greatest grievances, the necessity of supplying four times the amount of storage room that ought to be required. I have before me two books, one larger than the other in every way and four times as thick. Yet the smaller book is printed in larger type, has twice as many words on a page, and has twice as many pages. This is, of course, an exceptional contrast, but a difference of four times between the actual and the possible is by no means unusual. When one considers that in most of our libraries it costs, all told, a dollar to shelve a volume, one realizes that the librarian has against the publisher a grievance that can be put into the language of commerce. If every book is occupying a dollar's worth of space, which ought to accommodate three others, then, gentlemen publishers, in swelling your books to catch the public eye, you have taken from us far more than you put into your own pockets from your sales to us. You have made our book storage four times as costly and unwieldy as it ought to be; but you have done worse than this, you have sold us perishable instead of durable goods. You have cheapened every element of the book—paper, ink, and binding—so that, while we begin the twentieth century with some books on our shelves that are over four hundred years old and some that are less than one, the only books among them that have any chance of seeing the twenty-first century are those that will then be five hundred years old; the books that might have been a century old will then, like their makers, be dust. It seems to the librarian that you, who have taken it upon yourselves to direct the service to be rendered to men by the "art preservative of all arts," have assumed very lightly your responsibility for the future's knowledge of our time. You may and do answer that, as the records begin to perish, the most important of them will be reprinted, and the world will be the better off for the loss of the rest. To this it may be rejoined that you give the distant future no chance to revise the judgments of a rather near future, and that vast quantities of material which would be read with eagerness by future generations and which would be carefully preserved if it were durable, will not be reprinted, whatever its value. We may be sure that the daily papers of the present year will never be reprinted; the world of the future will be too busy, not to speak of the cost; yet what a series of human documents will disappear in their destruction! If a part of the professional obligation which you assumed in making yourselves responsible for the issues of the press is to transmit the record of this generation to later time, then it seems to me that you have in great measure betrayed your trust and have so far brought to naught the labors of your comrade, the librarian, in the conservation of literature. Also you compel him to pay for unnecessary rebindings which can hardly be made, so poor is the stock you furnish the binder; yet on this point you have shown some indications of a change of heart, and I will pass it over. Perhaps you have finally come to realize that every cent paid for rebinding is taken out of your gross receipts. I will not speak of the books that you ought never to have published, the books that are not books; most of these the librarian can avoid buying, but sometimes a book is just "ower gude for banning," and he has to take it and catalogue it and store it, and take account of it and rearrange it, and, after all, get scolded by his authorities or ridiculed by the public for housing so much rubbish. The author is responsible with you here, but your own individual responsibility is enough for any shoulders to bear.

To the printer the librarian would say: since wishing is easy, let us imagine that what ought always to happen is happening regularly instead of rarely, namely, that the author produces a book worth printing and that the publisher leaves you free to put it into a worthy form. This is the opportunity that you have always been looking for. How are you going to meet it? Do you know all the elements that you deal with and can you handle them with a sure touch practically and esthetically? If so, you will not need any hints from the librarian, and he will order your book "sight unseen." But still, among the good and right ways of making books, there may be some that he prefers, and he will ask you, when you are making books for him and not for private buyers, at least to give his preferences a hearing. He wants his books no bigger physically than they need be, and yet he would like to have them of a convenient height, from seven to nine inches. He would rather have their expansion in height and width and not in thickness, for the former dimensions up to ten and a half inches by eight mean no increased demand upon shelf room, while the thickness of every leaf is taken out of his library's capacity. He would like to have no wasteful margins and no extreme in the size of type. If it is too large, the book takes up too much room; if it is too small, his readers will ruin their eyes over it or, what is more likely, refuse to read it and so make its possession a useless expense. For the sake of rapid reading he would like to have every wide page printed in columns. For the same reason he would like to have every possible help given to the eye in the way of paragraphs, headlines, and variation of type, so far as it can be given in consonance with the esthetic rights of the book. With these points observed, and the book printed on paper as thin and as light in weight as can be conveniently used and is consistent with opacity and strength, with clear type, clear and durable ink, and good presswork, the printer will have done his part, and a book will go to the binder that is worthy of his best treatment.

What that treatment is the binder knows better than I can tell him. When he has applied it, the book will come out of his hands at once solid and flexible; unmutilated, either on the outer edges where mutilation can be seen, or at the back where it cannot be seen, but where it nevertheless hurts the integrity of the book; covered with honest boards that will stand use, and clad with a material, cloth or leather, that is both strong to resist wear and also contains within itself no seeds of deterioration. Besides this let it have a character, however unobtrusive, befitting the contents of the book, and the binder will have paid his full debt to the present and the future.

While the librarian's ideals of bookmaking are not the only ones, they are in harmony with the best, and there cannot be progress in bookmaking without approaching his ideals. He is, therefore, by his very office committed to every undertaking for the improvement of the book, and because of the efforts of librarians and other booklovers there is ground for belief that the books of the present decade will be better than those of the last.

THE BOOK BEAUTIFUL

WE who use books every day as tools of trade or sources of inspiration are apt to overlook the fact that the book, on its material side, is an art object. Not, indeed, that it ranks with the products of poetry, painting, sculpture, and other arts of the first grade; but it has a claim to our consideration on the level of the minor arts, along with jewelry, pottery, tapestry, and metal work. Moreover, its intimate association with literature, of which it is the visible setting, gives it a charm that, while often only reflected, may also be contributory, heightening the beauty that it enshrines.

Using the word beauty for the result of artistic mastery, we may say that in the other arts beauty is the controlling factor in price, but in the book this is the case only exceptionally. As a consequence beautiful books are more accessible for purchase or observation than any other equally beautiful objects. For the price of a single very beautiful rug one can obtain a small library of the choicest books. Except in the case of certain masterpieces of the earliest printing, in which rarity is joined to beauty, high prices for books have nothing to do with their artistic quality. Even for incunabula one need pay only as many dollars as for tapestries of the same grade one would have to pay thousands. In book collecting, therefore, a shallow purse is not a bar to achievement, and in our day of free libraries one may make good progress in the knowledge and enjoyment of beautiful books without any expense at all.

Public taste is probably as advanced in the appreciation of the book beautiful as of any other branch of art, but it is active rather than enlightened. This activity is a good sign, for it represents the first stage in comprehension; the next is the consciousness that there is more in the subject than had been realized; the third is appreciation. The present chapter is addressed to those—and they are many—who are in the second stage. The first piece of advice to those who seek acquaintance with the book beautiful is: Surround yourself with books that the best judges you know call beautiful; inspect them, handle them; cultivate them as you would friends. It will not be long before most other books begin to annoy you, though at first you cannot tell why. Then specific differences one after another will stand out, until at last you come to know something of the various elements of the book, their possibilities of beauty or ugliness, and their relations one to another. No one should feel ashamed if this process takes a long time—is indeed endless. William Morris pleaded to having sinned in the days of ignorance, even after he had begun to make books. So wide is the field and so many and subtle are the possible combinations that all who set out to know books must expect, like the late John Richard Green, to "die learning." But the learning is so delightful and the company into which it brings us is so agreeable that we have no cause to regret our lifelong apprenticeship.

The first of all the qualities of the book beautiful is fitness. It must be adapted to the literature which it contains, otherwise it will present a contradiction. Imagine a "Little Classic" Josephus or a folio Keats. The literature must also be worthy of a beautiful setting, else the book will involve an absurdity. Have we not all seen presentation copies of government documents which gave us a shock when we passed from the elegant outside to the commonplace inside? But the ideal book will go beyond mere fitness; it will be both an interpretation of its contents and an offering of homage to its worth. The beauty of the whole involves perfect balance as well as beauty of the parts. No one must take precedence of the rest, but there must be such a perfect harmony that we shall think first of the total effect and only afterwards of the separate elements that combine to produce it. This greatly extends our problem, but also our delight in its happy solutions.

The discerning reader has probably noticed that we have already smuggled into our introduction the notion that the book beautiful is a printed book; and, broadly speaking, so it must be at the present time. But we should not forget that, while the printed book has charms and laws of its own, the book was originally written by hand and in this form was developed to a higher pitch of beauty than the printed book has ever attained. As Ruskin says, "A well-written book is as much pleasanter and more beautiful than a printed book as a picture is than an engraving." Calligraphy and illumination are to-day, if not lost arts, at best but faint echoes of their former greatness. They represent a field of artistic effort in which many persons of real ability might attain far greater distinction and emolument than in the overcrowded ordinary fields of art. Printing itself would greatly benefit from a flourishing development of original bookmaking, gaining just that stimulus on the art side that it needs to counterbalance the pressure of commercialism. At present, however, we shall commit no injustice if, while remembering its more perfect original, we accept the printed book as the representative of the book beautiful; but, as a matter of fact, most that we shall have to say of it will apply with little change to the manuscript book.

A final point by way of preface is the relation of the book beautiful to the well-made book. The two are not identical. A book may be legible, strong, and durable, yet ill-proportioned and clumsy, ugly in every detail. On the other hand, the book beautiful must be well made, else it will not keep its beauty. The point where the two demands tend most to conflict is at the hinge of the cover, where strength calls for thickness of leather and beauty for thinness. The skill of the good binder is shown in harmonizing these demands when he shaves the under side of the leather for the joint. Let us now take up the elements of the book one by one and consider their relations to beauty.

To one who never had seen a book before it would seem, as it stands on the shelf or lies on the table, a curious rectangular block; and such it is in its origin, being derived from the Roman codex, which was a block of wood split into thin layers. When closed, therefore, the book must have the seeming solidity of a block; but open it and a totally new character appears. It is now a bundle of thin leaves, and its beauty no longer consists in its solidity and squareness, but in the opposite qualities of easy and complete opening, and flowing curves. This inner contradiction, so far from making the book a compromise and a failure, is one of the greatest sources of its charm, for each condition must be met as if the other did not exist, and when both are so met, we derive the same satisfaction as from any other combination of strength and grace, such as Schiller celebrates in his "Song of the Bell."

The book therefore consists of a stiff cover joined by a flexible back—in the book beautiful a tight back—and inclosing highly flexible leaves. The substance of the board is not visible, being covered with an ornamental material, either cloth or leather, but it should be strong and tough and in thickness proportioned to the size of the volume. In very recent years we have available for book coverings really beautiful cloths, which are also more durable than all but the best leathers; but we have a right to claim for the book beautiful a covering of leather, and full leather, not merely a back and hinges. We have a wide range of beauty in leathers, from the old ivory of parchment—when it has had a few centuries in which to ripen its color—to the sensuous richness of calf and the splendor of crushed levant. The nature of the book must decide, if the choice is yet to be made. But, when the book has been covered with appropriate leather so deftly that the leather seems "grown around the board," and has been lettered on the back—a necessary addition giving a touch of ornament—we are brought up against the hard fact that, unless the decorator is very skillful indeed—a true artist as well as a deft workman—he cannot add another touch to the book without lessening its beauty. The least obtrusive addition will be blind tooling, or, as in so many old books, stamping, which may emphasize the depth of color in the leather. The next step in the direction of ornament is gilding, the next inlaying. In the older books we find metal clasps and corners, which have great decorative possibilities; but these, like precious stones, have disappeared from book ornamentation in modern times before the combined inroad of the democratic and the classic spirit.

Having once turned back the cover, our interest soon forsakes it for the pages inclosed by it. The first of these is the page opposite the inside of the cover; obviously it should be of the same or, at least, of a similar material to the body of the book. But the inside of the cover is open to two treatments; it may bear the material either of the outer covering or of the pages within. So it may display, for instance, a beautiful panel of leather—doublure—or it may share with the next page a decorative lining paper; but that next page should never be of leather, for it is the first page of the book.

As regards book papers, we are to-day in a more fortunate position than we were even a few years ago; for we now can obtain, and at no excessive cost, papers as durable as those employed by the earliest printers. It is needless to say that these are relatively rough papers. They represent one esthetic advance in papermaking since the earliest days in that they are not all dead white. Some of the books of the first age of printing still present to the eye very nearly the blackest black on the whitest white. But, while this effect is strong and brilliant, it is not the most pleasing. The result most agreeable to the eye still demands black or possibly a dark blue ink, but the white of the paper should be softened. Whether we should have made this discovery of our own wit no one can tell; but it was revealed to us by the darkening of most papers under the touch of time. Shakespeare forebodes this yellowing of his pages; but what was then thought of as a misfortune has since been accepted as an element of beauty, and now book papers are regularly made "antique" as well as "white." Even white does not please us unless it inclines to creamy yellow rather than to blue. But here, as everywhere, it is easy to overstep the bounds of moderation and turn excess into a defect. The paper of the book beautiful will not attract attention; we shall not see it until our second look at the page. The paper must not be too thick for the size of the book, else the volume will not open well, and its pages, instead of having a flowing character, will be stiff and hard.

The sewing of the book is not really in evidence, except indirectly. Upon the sewing and gluing, after the paper, depends the flexibility of the book; but the sewing in most early books shows in the raised bands across the back, which are due to the primitive and preferable stitch. It may also show in some early and much modern work in saw-marks at the inner fold when the book is spread wide open; but no such book can figure as a book beautiful. The head band is in primitive books a part of the sewing, though in all modern books, except those that represent a revival of medieval methods, it is something bought by the yard and stuck in without any structural connection with the rest of the book.

It is the page and not the cover that controls the proportions of the book, as the living nautilus controls its inclosing shell. The range in the size of books is very great—from the "fly's-eye Dante" to "Audubon's Birds"—but the range in proportion within the limits of beauty is astonishingly small, a difference in the relation of the width of the page to its height between about sixty and seventy-five per cent. If the width is diminished to nearer one-half the height, the page becomes too narrow for beauty, besides making books of moderate size too narrow to open well. On the other hand, if the width is much more than three-quarters of the height, the page offends by looking too square. In the so-called "printer's oblong," formed by taking twice the width for the diagonal, the width is just under fifty-eight per cent of the height, and this is the limit of stately slenderness in a volume. As we go much over sixty per cent, the book loses in grace until we approach seventy-five per cent, when a new quality appears, which characterizes the quarto, not so much beauty, perhaps, except in small sizes, as a certain attractiveness, like that of a freight boat, which sets off the finer lines of its more elegant associates. A really square book would be a triumph of ugliness. Oblong books also rule themselves out of our category. A book has still a third element in its proportions, thickness. A very thin book may be beautiful, but a book so thick as to be chunky or squat is as lacking in elegance as the words we apply to it. To err on the side of thickness is easy; to err on the side of thinness is hard, since even a broadside may be a thing of beauty.

We now come to the type-page, of which the paper is only the carrier and framework. This should have, as nearly as possible, the proportion of the paper—really it is the type that should control the paper—and the two should obviously belong together. The margins need not be extremely large for beauty; an amount of surface equal to that occupied by the type is ample. There was once a craze for broad margins and even for "large-paper" copies, in which the type was lost in an expanse of margin; but book designers have come to realize that the proportion of white to black on a page can as easily be too great as too small. Far more important to the beauty of a page than the extent of the margin are its proportions. The eye demands that the upper margin of a printed page or a framed engraving shall be narrower than the lower, but here the kinship of page to picture ceases. The picture is seen alone, but the printed page is one of a pair and makes with its mate a double diagram. This consists of two panels of black set between two outer columns of white and separated by a column of white. Now if the outer and inner margins of a page are equal, the inner column of the complete figure will be twice as wide as the outer. The inner margin of the page should therefore be half (or, to allow for the sewing and the curve of the leaf, a little more than half) the width of the outer. Then, when we open the book, we shall see three columns of equal width. The type and paper pages, being of the same shape, should as a rule be set on a common diagonal from the inner upper corner to the outer lower corner. This arrangement will give the same proportion between the top and bottom margins as was assigned to the inner and outer. It is by attention to this detail that one of the greatest charms in the design of the book may be attained.

We saw that the shape of the book is a rectangle, and this would naturally be so if there were no other reason for it than because the smallest factor of the book, the type, is in the cross-section of its body a rectangle. The printed page is really built up of tiny invisible rectangles, which thus determine the shape of the paper page and of the cover. A page may be beautiful from its paper, its proportions, its color effects, even if it is not legible; but the book beautiful, really to satisfy us, must neither strain the eye with too small type nor offend it with fantastic departures from the normal. The size of the type must not be out of proportion to that of the page or the column; for two or more columns are not barred from the book beautiful. The letters must be beautiful individually and beautiful in combination. It has been remarked that while roman capitals are superb in combination, black-letter capitals are incapable of team play, being, when grouped, neither legible nor beautiful. There has been a recent movement in the direction of legibility that has militated against beauty of type, and that is the enlarging of the body of the ordinary lowercase letters at the expense of its limbs, the ascenders and descenders, especially the latter. The eye takes little account of descenders in reading, because it runs along a line just below the tops of the ordinary letters, about at the bar of the small e; nevertheless, to one who has learned to appreciate beauty in type design there is something distressing in the atrophied or distorted body of the g in so many modern types and the stunted p's and q's — which the designer clearly did not mind! The ascenders sometimes fare nearly as badly. Now types of this compressed character really call for leading, or separation of the lines; and when this has been done, the blank spaces thus created might better have been occupied by the tops and bottoms of unleaded lines containing letters of normal length and height. Too much leading, like too wide margins, dazzles and offends the eye with its excess of white. The typesetting machines have also militated against beauty by requiring that every letter shall stand within the space of its own feet or shoulders. Thus the lowercase f and y and the uppercase Q are shorn of their due proportions. These are points that most readers do not notice, but they are essential, for the type of the book beautiful must not be deformed by expediency. On the other hand, it need not be unusual; if it is, it must be exceptionally fine to pass muster at all. The two extremes of standard roman type, Caslon and Bodoni, are handsome enough for any book of prose. One may go farther in either direction, but at one's risk. For poetry, Cloister Oldstyle offers a safe norm, from which any wide departure must have a correspondingly strong artistic warrant. All these three types are beautiful, in their letters themselves, and in the combinations of their letters into lines, paragraphs, and pages. Beautiful typography is the very foundation of the book beautiful.

But beautiful typography involves other elements than the cut of the type itself. The proofreading must be trained and consistent, standing for much more than the mere correction of errors. The presswork must be strong and even. The justification must be individual for each line, and not according to a fixed scale as in machine setting; even when we hold the page upside down, we must not be able to detect any streamlets of white slanting across the page. Moreover, if the page is leaded, the spacing must be wider in proportion, so that the color picture of the rectangle of type shall be even and not form a zebra of black and white stripes. It is hardly necessary to say that the registration must be true, so that the lines of the two pages on the same leaf shall show accurately back to back when one holds the page to the light. Minor elements of the page may contribute beauty or ugliness according to their handling: the headline and page number, their character and position; notes marginal or indented, footnotes; chapter headings and initials; catchwords; borders, head and tail pieces, vignettes, ornamental rules. Even the spacing of initials is a task for the skilled craftsman. Some printers go so far as to miter or shave the type-body of initials to make them, when printed, seem to cling more closely to the following text. Indenting, above all in poetry, is a feature strongly affecting the beauty of the page. Not too many words may be divided between lines; otherwise the line endings will bristle with hyphens. A paragraph should not end at the bottom of a page nor begin too near it, neither should a final page contain too little nor be completely full. Minor parts of the book, the half-title, the dedication page, the table of contents, the preface, the index, present so many opportunities to make or mar the whole. Especially is this true of the title-page. This the earliest books did not have, and many a modern printer, confronted with a piece of refractory title copy, must have sighed for the good old days of the colophon. Whole books have been written on the title-page; it must suffice here to say that each represents a new problem, a triumphant solution of which gives the booklover as much pleasure to contemplate as any other single triumph of the volume.

But what of color — splendid initials in red, blue, or green, rubricated headings, lines, or paragraphs? It is all a question of propriety, literary and artistic. The same principle holds as in decoration of binding. A beautiful black and white page is so beautiful that he who would improve it by color must be sure of his touch. The beauty of the result and never the beauty of the means by itself must be the test.

But books are not always composed of text alone. We need not consider diagrams, which hardly concern the book beautiful, except to say that, being composed of lines, they are often really more decorative than illustrations fondly supposed to be artistic. The fact that an engraving is beautiful is no proof that it will contribute beauty to a book; it may only make an esthetic mess of the text and itself. As types are composed of firm black lines, only fairly strong black-line engravings have any artistic right in the book. This dictum, however, would rule out so many pictures enjoyed by the reader that he may well plead for a less sweeping ban; so, as a concession to weakness, we may allow white-line engravings and half-tones if they are printed apart from the text and separated from it, either by being placed at the end of the book or by having a sheet of opaque paper dividing each from the text. In this case the legend of the picture should face it so that the reader will have no occasion to look beyond the two pages when he has them before him. The printers of the sixteenth century, especially the Dutch, did not hesitate to send their pages through two presses, one the typographic press, and the other the roller press for copperplate engravings. The results give us perhaps the best example that we have of things beautiful in themselves but unlovely in combination. As in the use of other ornamental features, there are no bounds to the use of illustration except that of fitness.

We have spoken of margins from the point of view of the page; from that of the closed book they appear as edges, and here they present several problems in the design of the book beautiful. If the book is designed correctly from the beginning, the margins will be of just the right width and the edges cannot be trimmed without making them too narrow. Besides, the untrimmed edges are witnesses to the integrity of the book; if any exception may be made, it will be in the case of the top margin, which may be gilded both for beauty and to make easy the removal of dust. But the top should be rather shaved than trimmed, so that the margin may not be visibly reduced. The gilding of all the edges, or "full gilt," is hardly appropriate to the book beautiful, though it may be allowed in devotional books, especially those in limp binding, and its effect may there be heightened by laying the gilt on red or some other color. Edges may be goffered, that is, decorated with incised or burnt lines, though the result, like tattooing, is more curious than ornamental. The edges may even be made to receive pictures, but here again the effect smacks of the barbaric.

We have now gone over our subject in the large. To pursue it with all possible degrees of minuteness would require volumes. William Morris, for instance, discusses the proper shape for the dot of the i; and even the size of the dot and its place above the letter are matters on which men hold warring opinions. We have not even raised the question of laid or wove paper, nor of the intermixture of different series or sizes of types. In short, every phase of the subject bristles with moot points, the settlement of one of which in a given way may determine the settlement of a score of others.

But what is the use to the public of this knowledge and enjoyment of ours? Is it not after all a fruitless piece of self-indulgence? Surely, if bookmaking is one of the minor arts, then the private knowledge and enjoyment of its products is an element in the culture of the community. But it is more than that; it is both a pledge and a stimulus to excellence in future production. Artists in all fields are popularly stigmatized as a testy lot—*irritabile genus*—but their techiness does not necessarily mean opposition to criticism, but only to uninformed and unappreciative criticism, especially if it be cocksure and blatant. There is nothing that the true artist craves so much—not even praise—as understanding of his work and the welcome that awaits his work in hand from the lips of "those who know." Thus those who appreciate and welcome the book beautiful, by their encouragement help to make it more beautiful, and so by head and heart, if not by hand, they share in the artist's creative effort. Also, by thus promoting beauty in books, they discourage ugliness in books, narrowing the public that will accept ugly books and lessening the degree of ugliness that even this public will endure. Finally, it seems no mere fancy to hold that by creating the book beautiful as the setting of the noblest literature, we are rendering that literature itself a service in the eyes of others through the costly tribute that we pay to the worth of the jewel itself.

THE READER'S HIGH PRIVILEGE

IN De Morgan's winsome story, "Alice for Short," the heroine of the earlier portion, Miss Peggy Heath, is made to feel what it would mean to her to be deprived of a certain companion, and thus realizes his importance to her life.

It is this test of elimination that I shall ask you to apply to reading. Imagine yourselves deprived of the privilege, as many another has been by loss of sight or illness or poverty or removal from book centers. I have in mind such an instance. The late Professor William Mathews was injured by a fall when he was ninety years old, and until the end of his life, about a year later, was confined to his bed. You may know him as the author of various books of essays: "Getting on in the World," "Great Conversers," "Hours with Men and Books," "Words, their Use and Abuse," and other volumes that testify a marvelous range of acquaintance with literature. He wrote to a friend that he was brightening his hours of loneliness by repeating to himself passages of poetry and prose that he had learned by heart in his earlier days. Few of us can ever have such stores of memory to draw upon as his, but how happy we should be if under such circumstances we might be able to turn to a like source of consolation. Yet we have a much more famous instance of a great scholar cut off from the privilege of reading. Milton has given us in his famous invocation to Light, with which he opens the third book of "Paradise Lost," a picture of his own deprivation, presented with a universal blank in place of Nature's fair book of knowledge. The passage is too long to quote here, but let the reader turn to it, if only to refresh his memory.

This shows the privilege that we are now enjoying, and it may perhaps be sufficient to take our lesson at this point; but since it is always pleasanter to consider gain rather than loss, suppose we turn the subject around and imagine how it would seem if, after having been deprived all our lives of the privilege of reading, we suddenly had it thrust upon us. We should now find ourselves able to enjoy those wonderful works of literature which we had always been hearing about from the lips of others, but had never been able to know directly. How we should revel in the prospect before us! At last to be able to read the "Iliad"! To follow the fortunes of wandering Ulysses! To accompany Dante in his mystical journey through the three worlds! To dare with Macbeth and to doubt with Hamlet! Our trouble would be that we should not know which to select first. We should wish we had the eyes of an insect that we might read them all at once.

We have a familiar expression in taking leave of our friends, "Be good to yourself!" which, it will be seen, is the modern man's translation of the old "farewell," with the truly modern implication that the question of his faring well will depend upon himself. But can we call a man good to himself who does not avail himself of advantages that are freely open to him and that others about him are embracing? The great men of the past have been such because to their natural abilities they added an acquaintance with the thought of the great men who preceded them. The same is true of the men whom we are glad to honor among our contemporaries. We may feel very sure that we are not heaven-descended geniuses, or even possessed of unusual talent; and yet, if we do not give ourselves the advantages that all those had who have won distinction, we have certainly not given ourselves a fair chance to show what is in us. Therefore, as a duty to ourselves, we must make the acquaintance of the books that the common judgment of the world has pronounced to be of the most value. They must become more than names to us. We may not indeed find in all of them food for our own spirits, but it is a part of our business in seeking a knowledge of mankind to know the thoughts and thought-forms that men have found of most worth. It is not to be supposed that we shall prize all these books equally; some of them will never be more to us than great monuments which, for some reason peculiar to our temperaments, do not appeal to us; but among their number we shall find some that will throw open to our souls the very gates of heaven—books that will raise our natures forevermore to a higher power, as if from two-dimensional Flatland creatures we had suddenly been advanced to three dimensions, or, in our own humdrum world of length, breadth, and thickness, we had received the liberty of the mysterious fourth dimension.

Let us now take a brief inventory of our heritage. We can glance at only the most precious of these treasures, the crown jewels of the world's literature, which are all ours, whether we choose to wear them or not. But first let me make it plain that I am not assuming that all the great monuments of human genius are literary. I am not forgetful of the fact that literature is only one of the fine arts, that the Strassburg Cathedral, Beethoven's Ninth Symphony, Rembrandt's School of Anatomy, Michelangelo's Moses are all products of man's creative genius, records of the life of God in the soul of man. But I do insist that literature is the most inclusive and the most definite of all the arts, and that therefore books unlock to us a vaster world than obeys the spell of any other art. One man's soul may attain its transfiguration through architecture or music or painting or sculpture as another does through poetry; the great thing is to attain the transfiguration; and let us be thankful for the many ways in which God fulfills himself to man. I am not trying to make out a case for literature, but literature is my subject, and what I say of it must be taken as equally friendly to all the other great forms of human expression and often as equally applicable to them.

We will not talk of a five-foot or a three-foot shelf, or one of any other exact dimension, though I suspect that no very long range of space would be required to hold all the supremely great books for whose contents we should have room in our souls. The limitation will prove to be in us rather than in the material of literature. The Bible, while containing supremely great literature, has still higher claims, and for the present discussion may be left to its special advocates. But meanwhile our treasures are waiting for their inventory.

Literature for people of our race begins with Homer and is confined to Europe and English America. This means in a very true sense that all the literature which concerns us is modern, for the Greeks are the first and perhaps the greatest of the moderns. They present us as their first contribution the works that go under the name of Homer, and we need not disturb ourselves now with the question whether the "Iliad" and the "Odyssey" were both written by the same man, or even each written by a single hand. The point is that we have in them an imperishable picture of the life of a vanished world. Each is an epic of the natural man, the one national, the other personal. In the "Iliad" we are plunged into the thickening close of the ten years' war between the Greeks and Trojans, during which the beautiful cause of all the trouble, Helen, retains all her youthful bloom and, in fact, nobody seems to grow any older. We have a crowded stage with many episodes and interests. In the "Odyssey" we trace the fortunes of one man, Ulysses, during his return from the war, which occupies him ten years, so that he is away from home, as Rip Van Winkle was, twenty years; but, instead of finding everybody grown old or dead, as Irving's hero did, he finds his wife still young and attractive and beset by numerous suitors. We are very glad to have this so, because we are all children at heart and want just such an ending. The telling of these stories, while simple, is on a lofty plane; the gods themselves take part in the passions of the contestants and even in the warfare. The poet, no doubt, meant this for what it professes to be; but I cannot help seeing in the embroiling of Olympus a perhaps unrealized tribute of the poet to the greatness of the human soul in the scale of the universe, a suggestion that moral and spiritual values and powers outweigh the stars in their courses.

Great as are the works of Homer, we are not to suppose them the only masterpieces in Greek literature. Certainly the three great dramatists cannot be omitted, all so great, yet so unlike. These three, together with two pastoral poets, one lyric poet, and the greatest of prose poets, are vividly pictured by Mrs. Browning in the glowing stanzas of her "Wine of Cyprus."

> Oh, our Æschylus, the thunderous!
> How he drove the bolted breath
> Through the cloud, to wedge the ponderous
> In the gnarlèd oak beneath.
> Oh, our Sophocles, the royal,
> Who was born to monarch's place,

And who made the whole world loyal,
  Less by kingly power than grace.
Our Euripides, the human,
  With his droppings of warm tears,
And his touches of things common
  Till they rose to touch the spheres!
Our Theocritus, our Bion,
  And our Pindar's shining goals!—
These were cup-bearers undying
  Of the wine that's meant for souls.
And my Plato, the divine one,
  If men know the gods aright
By their motions as they shine on
  With a glorious trail of light!—

It would not be surprising if some who read these lines should find more food for mind and soul in Plato than in any other of the Greek writers. Certainly those works of Plato and his contemporary, Xenophon, that relate to the life, teachings, and death of Socrates are contributions to a yet uncollected Bible of humanity, one more inclusive than that of Jew or Christian.

It is one of the great misfortunes of Roman literature that the works of its chief writers are used as textbooks for schools, a misfortune shared to some extent by the Greek. Yet Homer and Xenophon, Vergil and Cicero, did not write for children or callow youth. They belong to Longfellow's

grand old masters,
Whose mighty thoughts suggest
Life's endless toil and endeavor,

and their writings have no relation to adolescence. Yet it is to be feared that most people who have read their works remember them as seen through the cloudy medium of their own immaturity. Byron speaks of reading and hating Horace as a schoolboy, but no normal person can hate Horace any more than he can hate Washington Irving. It is possible, however, that pupils who have to read Irving's

"Sketch Book" with the fear of a college entrance examination before their minds may have no affection even for him. So some of us may have something to unlearn in our reading of Vergil and Horace, for we must approach their works as strong meat for mature minds. Vergil's theme is nothing less than the glorification of the Roman state through its divinely ordered and heroic founding. School children seldom read more than the six books of the "Aeneid" required for college; but the other six, though of much less varied interest, are necessary for the appreciation of the poem. The whole is a work that no one can afford to pass over in his search for the burning words that keep alive the thought of other ages. Very different in theme and manner is the poetry of Horace. He is the most modern of all the men of old, far more modern than our own Puritan ancestors. His mixture of grace and shrewdness, poetic charm and worldly wisdom, we find nowhere else. The bulk of his work is not large, and this fact, as in the case of Gray and Keats and Poe, is rather in his favor, because the reader can easily become familiar with it all, though then he will sigh for more. Horace wears well; the older we grow the better we like him. He has love songs for youth, political poems for maturity, and satires for old age. After we have lived with him for half a century he becomes more real to us than most of our acquaintances in the flesh. Roman literature is not without other great names to attract the student; but these two must not be overlooked by the most general or the most selective reader.

With Vergil the world always associates the still greater figure of one who was proud to call him master—that of Dante. More than is true of almost any other writer, his work is a compendium of the life of his time. The "Divine Comedy" is first of all poetry, and poetry of the loftiest order; but it is also an embodiment of the learning, the philosophy, and the theology of his age. It mirrors at once the greatness and the limitations of the medieval mind. Dante is not modern in the sense that Horace is, though he is thrice as near to us in time. Leigh Hunt said that his great poem ought to be called an infernal tragedy; but that is true only of the Inferno; the spiritual atmosphere clears as we follow his footsteps through the Purgatorio and the Paradiso. Of all the masterpieces of human genius the "Divine Comedy" is perhaps the one that asks the most self-surrender of the modern reader and—shall I add?—that repays it most richly. Longfellow's marvelous sonnet sequence, written while he was translating Dante, portrays at once the spirit in which we should approach the reading of the "Divine Comedy" and the wonders that we shall find there. It is a book that we never can outgrow. To know it is to be made a citizen of the moral universe.

In 1616, within ten days of each other, there passed from earth two men, each the writer first thought of when his country's literature is mentioned, and one of them the first writer in the world's literature. Cervantes and Shakespeare very likely died in ignorance of each other's work. Stoddard has depicted them in Paradise,

> Where sweet Cervantes walks,
> A smile on his grave face . . .
> Where, little seen but light,
> The only Shakespeare is.

There is no injustice in saying that Shakespeare's nature included that of Cervantes. Not so inclusive was Dante's; what his nature most lacked we find in the author of "Don Quixote." Yet personally they are equally heroic figures, and, one an exile and the other a slave, both drained to the dregs the cup of human suffering. Cervantes has several great advantages over most of the world's classic writers: his masterpiece is a work of humor; it is written in a simple and graceful style, at once easy and winning; and it is written in prose, which, after all, does not make so severe a cultural demand on the reader as poetry. For these very reasons it cannot aspire to the highest rank, but what it loses in fame it makes up in popularity. Though in a few passages it is not parlor reading, "Don Quixote" is one of the cleanest of all the world's great books. It is not merely technically clean, but clean-minded. It has the form of a satire on chivalry, but its meaning goes much deeper. It is really a satire on a more persistent weakness of the Spanish character, visionary unrealism. We have this quality held up to ridicule in the learned man and the ignorant man, for Sancho Panza is as much of an unrealist as his master, only he is a groveling visionary while Don Quixote is a soaring one. This, too, is a book that one does not outgrow, but finds it a perpetually adequate commentary on his own widening experience of men and their motives.

In regard to the supreme figure in literature, the least thing that we can do is to read him, and, having read him, to read him again and to keep his volumes next to our hands. We shall hardly read Shakespeare without having the question of commentators come up; and surely Shakespeare deserves all the attention that we can bestow upon him. But the general reader should clearly distinguish between the two kinds of commentary that have appeared regarding Shakespeare, the one having to do with his text, his historical accuracy, and his use of words, the other with his meaning. In Hudson's edition these two kinds of notes are kept separate. Surely it is the thought of Shakespeare that we want, and not the pedantry of minute scholarship regarding his material, useful as that is in its place. The reader who has mastered Hudson's introductions and has read Dowden's "Shakspere: His Mind and Art" or Brandes's "Critical Study" will have all that he will ordinarily need in the way of guidance. But remember that reading about Shakespeare is not reading Shakespeare; *that* means, for the time at least, self-surrender to Shakespeare's leading. Shakespeare is perhaps the supreme example of a man who found the world interesting. He may not be sympathetic with evil, but he finds it so interesting that he makes us, for the time being, take a fratricidal usurper like Hamlet's uncle, or a gross, sponging braggart like Falstaff, at his own estimate. Shakespeare is never shocked at anything that happens in the world; he knows the world too well for that. He offends the Puritan in us by his indifference; he is therefore probably the best kind of reading for Puritans. Shakespeare is romantic in his literary methods, but in his portrayal of character he is an unsurpassed realist. If life were all thought and achievement, Shakespeare would be the last word in literature; but there is another side, the side which the Puritan represents, with which Shakespeare is but imperfectly sympathetic. His message accordingly needs to be supplemented; and it is interesting that his great successor, the man who still stands next to him in our literature, supplies that missing strain. If we could take but one book with us into banishment, it would be Shakespeare—thus proving Shakespeare's supremacy by Miss Peggy Heath's principle of elimination; but if we could take two, that second, I am frank to confess, would for me be Milton.

It is Milton's literary glory that he appeared in the second generation following Spenser and Shakespeare — he was born in Shakespeare's lifetime — and carried off the palm, which he still keeps, for the greatest English poem. In spiritual kinship he is much nearer to Spenser than to

Shakespeare. Shakespeare hides behind his pages; his personality makes no clear or at least ready impression upon us; but the colossal personality of Milton towers above all his works. He is Milton, the superman, and communion with him for the moment lifts us to something like his own level. In this personal inspiration lies Milton's greatest service to his readers. Over and above the poetic delights, of which he is a master unsurpassed, is the inspiration that comes from the man behind the poetry; or, to express the same thought in other words, above the organ music of his verse sounds clear and far the trumpet call of personality. Therefore Milton is destined to inspire generations by which his theology and his justification of the ways of God to man are swept into his own limbo of myth and delusion. Fortunately Milton's verse is not appallingly great in amount. If we cannot hope to know it all by heart, as Macaulay did, we can at least know it well enough to recognize any quotation from it, and rich will be the furnishing of our minds when we have made this true.

In our beadroll of the world's greatest writers I shall mention only one more, Goethe. He is the modern man who touched life most widely, penetratingly, and sanely. His long life came down so near to ours that many of us have had friends who were in childhood or infancy his contemporaries. It is fair to say that since his death the world has moved much nearer to his mental attitude than it stood in his lifetime, and one of the agencies that have wrought the change is the living force of his own works, which led and still lead the thought of men. Goethe may be called the ideal creative critic of life. He held up a mirror, not to Nature, as Shakespeare did, but to society; and society can get away from the image which it sees reflected there only by growing away from it.

Here let us close our list, not because there are no other great writers to choose from, but because it is long enough for our present purposes, and because, from this point on, every addition is open to challenge. I have intentionally pitched my counsel high; some of my readers may feel like calling it a counsel of perfection; but according to my way of thinking, no writer is too good for any of us to read. Moreover, I honestly think the list interesting. It is not chiefly reading for recreation, but for soul expansion, and it means intellectual effort. Unless we wrestle with an author as Jacob did with the angel, we shall not receive the highest blessing. But some one may plead that, while he does not wish to read wholly for amusement, he is not in a condition, either from training or circumstances, to engage in mental athletics. He cannot apply himself to an author as he recognizes that the greatest writers deserve; but he is willing to read with attention, and he should like to feel that what he is reading is good literature. This is a reasonable request, and, out of countless possible responses, I will make one that I hope may prove both profitable and attractive.

Let us set out with the recognition of the fact that systematic reading is far more profitable than desultory reading, even on the same literary level. One excellent way to achieve system is to read by authors—to make the author a study, in his writings and his life. To read Hawthorne's "House of the Seven Gables," for instance, is to drink from a fountain of the purest spiritual delight; but we gain an additional delight, even if of a lower kind, when we know something of Hawthorne's life and his relations to the old town of Salem. In many cases it is necessary to know the author's life in order really to understand his book. Now I will suggest the reading, not merely of separate authors, but of a group. There are many such, of varying degrees of greatness: the Elizabethan group, the Lake poets, the Byron-Shelley-Keats group, the mid-nineteenth-century British novelists, to go no further than writers in English. But I am going to ask your interest in the New England group of authors who were writing fifty years ago. They comprise the well-known names of Emerson, Hawthorne, Longfellow, Whittier, Holmes, Thoreau, and Lowell. Each of these delightful writers deserves to be studied for his own sake, but, if we take them as a group, we shall gain still more in understanding and profit. How shall we approach the reading of them? They obviously cannot all be read at once; so let us begin with any one, say Hawthorne, read his life in Mrs. Field's brief Beacon Biography, dipping at the same time into his "Note-Books," and then read some of his short stories and the "Scarlet Letter." His biography will already have brought us into contact with most of the other names, of Longfellow, his college classmate, and of Emerson and Thoreau, his neighbors at Concord. We may read the Beacon Biography of Longfellow, but Higginson's would be better, as fuller and more adequate. We may first read Longfellow's prose works, "Outre-Mer" and "Hyperion," and then his "Voices of the Night," besides following him in his "Life, with Extracts from his Journal and Correspondence," edited by his brother, which is one of the most delightful of books. We shall do well to read each author's writings in chronological succession; so they will stand in orderly relation with his life. Similarly we may take up Emerson first in Mr. Sanborn's Beacon Biography, or in Dr. Holmes's larger but still handy volume, and then we can apply ourselves with better understanding to Emerson's essays and poems. I particularly mention his poems, for I believe that Emerson will come to be rated higher as a poet than he has yet been. His poetry at its best is hardly below anyone's best;

the only trouble is that there is so little of it; but ultimately all writers are judged by their best. In the same way we may take up all the writers of the group, learning something of the life of each and reading some of his works before passing on to another. Let me especially call your attention to the writings of Thoreau, who is less known to his countrymen than any of the others. He is a writer of great originality and freshness of view. He, too, wrote some exquisite poetry, worthy of any name in literature; but you will have to look for it among other verse that has more originality than charm. Obviously what I have recommended is not the work of one year's leisure, but the protracted delight of many years: for these books are not to be hurried over to get to the end of the chapter or to see how they are coming out; neither are they material for skipping. They are to be read attentively and reread; and if one or another fails to make a strong appeal to some reader, surely he cannot fail to find in most of them a source of lofty pleasure and spiritual enrichment. One fruit that we may expect from such reading is that we shall find ourselves drawn nearer to the supreme masters and shall end by surrendering ourselves to them. To know our New England group is not indeed to climb the Alps of literature, but it is at least to climb its White Mountains. Every gain will be a fresh incitement, and those who at the start join the literary Appalachian Club may be looked for some day in the ranks of the Alpinists.

A word on the reading of contemporary writers; for even our second list did not bring us down to our own time. We shall, of course, read our contemporaries, and we have a right to, so long as we do not give them the time and attention that clearly belong to their betters. The truth is that contemporaries—unless they are contemporary poets—have a quite unfair advantage over their elders, our own in time and place being so much more attractive to us than anything more remote. Still, our contemporaries have a claim upon us—even, I am rash enough to assert, our contemporary poets—for they have a message that their predecessors cannot give us; it may not be the most important message for us, but it is a message of value, as we shall see if we return to De Morgan and his novels. These remarkable books we cannot miss without losing something that makes our own day fine and precious among earth's generations. But in this respect they are literally chosen from ten thousand, for we need constantly the caution that the near carries with it an appearance of importance that is an illusion; of this truth our periodical literature, from the newspaper up, is the illustrious example, and the lesson is all summed up in the one phrase, "back number." Let us be careful that in heeding contemporary voices we are not storing our minds with the contents of "back numbers." True literature as we have seen, never becomes out of date; Homer keeps up with the telegraph.

I have but one final word, which has been provided for me by Charles Lamb, who says in his inimitable fashion: "I own that I am disposed to say grace upon twenty other occasions in the course of the day besides my dinner. I want a form for setting out upon a pleasant walk, for a moonlight ramble, for a friendly meeting, or a solved problem. Why have we none for books, those spiritual repasts —a grace before Milton—a grace before Shakespeare—a devotional exercise proper to be said before reading the Fairy Queen?" This is the spirit of a joyous but devoutly grateful expectance, in which I would have myself approach the reading of a great book. The gratitude I surely owe the author, for there is no great book but has come like refined gold out of the furnace fire. I owe it also to the Providence which has granted me this lofty privilege. Moreover, it is only in the humility born of such an attitude that I can make a complete approach to my author and gain that uplift and enrichment of the soul, which—and not pastime nor pleasure—is the true end, as it should be the aim of reading.

THE BACKGROUND OF THE BOOK

ONE of the greatest contributions that modern investigation has made to human knowledge is background. It was once thought a remarkable achievement to uncover the historic background of modern institutions, and this was all that, until lately, scholarship attempted. Dr. Samuel Johnson confidently remarked that we know no more about ancient Britain than the old writers have told us, nor can we ever know any more than this. Edward Clodd reminds us that at the very time when the great oracle voiced this assertion discoveries had already been made in England that, when interpreted as they have been since, were to make the landing of Caesar seem, by comparison, a contemporary occurrence. Now this inconceivably remote prehistoric era furnishes not merely arrowheads and stone chisels and burial mounds, but also other objects that are the background of that "picture of time" of which the book of to-day is the foreground.

Very properly these are objects of art, and they afford the earliest illustrations in histories of art as they do in histories of the book. Thus the printer who questions what art has to do with his business stamps himself as two hundred thousand years behind the times. They are pictures, and the book of to-day has descended as directly from them as the printer of to-day has descended from the man who made them. They are, moreover, in some instances, works of very high art. The picture of the mammoth, scratched on a fragment of the mammoth's tusk, is a piece of drawing so skillful that only the greatest living masters can equal it. Not even Rembrandt's drawing of the elephant, which Dr. Holmes celebrates in one of his poems, is more expressive or wrought with more economy of effort. In the same district of southwestern France, Dordogne, that yielded the drawings are found long cave galleries of paintings representing the creatures of that period, all executed with great spirit and ability. But what are the steps in the descent from these ancient pictures to the printed book?

Primitive man had one more string to his conversational bow than most civilized people have, namely, sign language. But gesture and speech alike prevail but little against space and time. Each is possible only at short range, and each dies on the eye or ear that receives it. Pictures may be carried to any distance and may be preserved for any length of time. They were probably made first in response to an instinct rather for art than for the communication of ideas; but their great advantage for communication must have been perceived very early, and, as we find picture writing employed by primitive races to-day, we have the right to infer that prehistoric peoples at the same stage of culture also employed it. Pure picture writing, however, does not suffice for all that men have to say. It is easy to represent a house, but how shall we represent a home? It is easy to represent a woman, but how shall we add the idea of wife? To do this we must pass from simple pictures to symbols. Chinese writing has never advanced beyond this stage. Its prodigious type-case of more than forty-two thousand characters contains, therefore, only a series of pictures, direct and symbolic, all highly conventionalized, but recognizable in their earlier forms. To represent "wife" the Chinaman combines the two signs for "woman" and "broom"; to represent "home" he makes a picture of a pig under a roof! The Egyptian and Mexican systems of writing, though very different to the eye, were both of this nature and represented ideas rather than words. Yet all true alphabets, which are representations of sound, have been derived from such primitive ideograms or pictures of ideas. What was the process?

The rebus is the bridge from the writing of thoughts to the writing of sounds, and it came into use through the necessity of writing proper names. Every ancient name, like many modern ones, had a meaning. A king's name might be Wolf, and it would be indicated by the picture of a wolf. Ordinarily the picture would be named by everyone who saw it according to his language; he might call it "wolf," or "lupus," or "lykos"; but when it meant a man's name he must call it Wolf, whatever his own language. So such names as Long Knife and Strong Arm would be represented, and these pictures would thus be associated with the sound rather than the thing. By and by it was found convenient, where the word had several syllables, to use its picture to represent the sound of only the first syllable, and, still later, of only the first sound or letter. Thus the Egyptian symbol for F was originally a picture of the horned asp, later it stood for the Egyptian name of this venomous creature, and finally for the first sound in the name, being used as the letter F itself; and the reason why we have the barred cross-piece in the F, the two horns in U, V, and Y, and the four in W (VV) is because the Egyptian asp had two horns, as may be seen from the illustration in the Century Dictionary under the word cerastes; and every time that we write one of these letters we are making a faded copy of the old picture. We find systems of writing in all the stages from pure pictures to the phonetic alphabet; in Egyptian hieroglyphics we find a mixture of all the stages. So much for the background of the book as the bringer of a message to the eye, but the outward form or wrapping of that message has also a long and interesting history.

No objects could be much more unlike than a Babylonian tablet, an Egyptian papyrus roll, and a Mexican book. They are as different as a brick, a narrow window-shade, and a lady's fan; they have nothing common in their development, yet they were used for the same purpose and might bring identically the same message to the mind. Inwardly, as regards writing or printing, all books have a parallel development; but outwardly, in their material and its form, they are the results of local conditions. In Babylonia, which was a fertile river-bottom, bricks were the only building material, and clay was therefore a familiar substance. Nothing was more natural than that the Babylonian should scratch his record or message on a little pat of clay, which he could afterwards bake and render permanent. Some day all other books in the world will have crumbled into dust, their records being saved only when reproduced; but at that remote time there will still exist Babylonian books, even now five thousand years old, apparently no nearer destruction than when they were first made.

The Babylonian book carried its message all on the outside; the Egyptian book went to the opposite extreme, and we should find our chief objection to it in the difficulty of getting readily at its contents. There flourished on the banks of the Nile a stout reed, six feet high, called by the Egyptians "p-apa" and by the Greeks "papyros" or "byblos." It was the great source of raw material for Egyptian manufactures. Its tufted head was used for garlands; its woody root for various purposes; its tough rind for ropes, shoes, and similar articles — the basket of Moses, for instance; and its cellular pith for a surface to write on. As the stem was jointed, the pith came in lengths, the best from eight to ten inches. These lengths were sliced through from top to bottom, and the thin slices laid side by side. Another layer was pasted crosswise above these, the whole pressed, dried in the sun, and rubbed smooth, thus giving a single sheet of papyrus. As the grain ran differently on the two surfaces of the papyrus sheet, only one side was written on. Other sheets were added to this by pasting them edge to edge until enough for a roll had been made, usually twenty, a roller being fastened to the last edge and a protecting strip of wood to the front. The manuscript was unrolled by the right hand and rolled up by the left. It is obvious that a book of reference in this form would be subjected to great wear. In our dictionaries it is as easy to find Z as A; but in a papyrus book, to find the end meant to unroll the whole. The Latin word for roll was "volumen," hence our "volume." A long work could obviously not be produced conveniently in a single roll, therefore Homer's "Iliad" and "Odyssey," for instance, were each divided into twenty-four books, and that is why the divisions of an epic poem are still called books, though they are really chapters. The rolls composing a single work were kept together in a case something like a bandbox. The roll was the book form of the Greek and Roman as well as the Egyptian world, but it left no descendants. Our book form was derived from a different source, which we will now consider.

Just as we speak of Russia leather, so the ancients spoke of Pergamum skins, or parchment. The story is that Eumenes II, King of Pergamum, a city of Asia Minor, tried to build up a library rivaling that of Alexandria, and the Ptolemies, seeking to thwart him, forbade the export of papyrus from Egypt. Eumenes, however, developed the manufacture of Pergamum skin, or parchment, or vellum, which not only enabled him to go on with his library, but also incidentally changed the whole character of the book for future ages. This material is not only much more serviceable than the fragile papyrus, but, being tough enough to stand folding and sewing, permitted the book to be made in its present or codex form, the original codex being two or three Roman waxed tablets of wood, fastened together like hinged slates, and thus opening very crudely in the manner of our books. This development of parchment occurred in the first half of the second century before Christ. The new material and book form gradually made their way into favor and came to constitute the book of the early Christian and medieval world. Though paper was introduced into Europe soon after the year seven hundred, it did not displace parchment until the invention of printing called for a material of its cheaper and more adaptable character.

But, though we have traced the origin of our present book form, we have not yet filled in the background of its history. Several other notable types of the book deserve our attention; first of all that of China, one of the most attractive of all book forms, to which we devote our next chapter. Though it superficially resembles our own books, it is really the product of a different line of evolution. When we examine it closely, we find that in many respects it is the exact reverse of our practice. It is printed on only one side of the paper; it is trimmed at the back and folded on the fore edge; its wide margin is at the top; its running headline is on the folded fore edge; its sewing is on the outside; its binding is limp; its lines run up and down the page; and its pages, according to Western ideas, open from the back towards the front. Yet it is a thing of beauty, and let us hope that nothing in the modern reorganization of China will change its character to prevent it from remaining a joy forever.

Just as Chinese paper is made from bamboo, which plays an even greater part in China than papyrus did in Egypt, so the book of India utilizes the leaves of that important tropical tree, the palm. The sheets of the book before me are strips of palm-leaf two inches wide and two feet long. They are written on both sides and, following the run of the grain, lengthwise. This makes an inordinate length of line, but, owing to the small number of lines on the page, the confusion of the eye is less than might be expected. The leaves composing the book are clamped between two boards of their own size, the block thus formed is pierced with two holes, through which pins are thrust, and the whole is wound with a cord. The dimensions vary, some books being larger and some much smaller. I have also before me a Burmese booklet in which the leaves are one inch wide and six inches long. Sometimes the sheets are of brass, beautifully lacquered, and the writing heavy and highly decorative. These books also vary greatly in size, some forming truly massive and sumptuous volumes. Birch bark was also employed as a book material in India, being used in what we should call quarto sheets, and in Farther India a peculiar roll is in use, made of Chinese paper, folded at the side, sewed at the top, and rolled up like a manifold banner in a cover of orange-colored or brown cotton cloth.

We do not ordinarily associate books with pre-Columbian America; yet one of the most interesting of all book forms was current in Mexico before the Conquest. As in the case of the Chinese book, it looks superficially like ours; we think it is a tiny quarto until we see that its measure is rather that of an oblong twenty-fourmo; that is, its dimensions are just scant of five inches high and six inches wide. It has thin wooden covers and is, over all, an inch thick; but between these covers is a strip of deerskin twenty-nine feet long and, of course, nearly five inches wide. This is folded in screen or fan fashion, the first and last leaves being pasted to the inside of the covers. This attachment is really the only binding; the whole strip is capable of being opened up to its full length. It is read—by those who can read its vividly colored hieroglyphics—by holding it like a modern book, turning the leaves until what seems the end is reached, and then turning the cover for the next leaf, and continuing to turn until the first cover is reached again, but from the other side. Incredible as it may seem, there is a book of India which is almost identical in structure with the ancient Mexican book. It has the shape of the palm-leaf book, but it is made of heavy paper, blackened to be written on with a chalk pencil, and it opens like a fan exactly in the Mexican fashion. Each cover is formed by a double fold of paper, and the writing runs lengthwise of the page as in the palm-leaf volume. As the writing can be erased, the book serves the purpose of a slate.

The variety of objects that men have used to write upon almost surpasses imagination, ranging from mountain walls to the ivory shoulders of Rider Haggard's heroine in his "Mr. Meeson's Will." Such unusual, if actual, writing materials belong, perhaps, rather to the penumbra than to the background of the book; but, as a final survey of our subject, running back to the time when there were no books and men must rely upon their memories, we may quote what Lane says of the sources from which the Kuran was derived after the death of Mohammed: "So Zeyd gathered the Kurán from palm-leaves, skins, shoulder-blades (of beasts), stones, and the hearts of men."

THE CHINESE BOOK

THE naturalist, Lloyd Morgan, in one of his lectures threw together on the screen pictures of a humming bird and an insect of the same size, the two looking so much alike as to seem to the casual observer to belong to the same order. Yet they are anatomically far more different than the man and the fish. In much the same way we may be led to suppose that a Chinese book and an occidental paper-bound book are much the same thing in origin as they are to the eye. But here too the likeness is only apparent. One book form has descended from a block of wood and the other from a fold of silk.

The Chinese book is such a triumph of simplicity, cheapness, lightness, and durability that it deserves a more careful study at the hands of our book producers than it has yet received. In fact we do not see why books made on nearly these lines should not be an attractive and popular innovation in our book trade. Approaches, to be sure, have been made to this peculiar book form, but they have been partial imitations, not consistent reproductions. In an illustrated edition of Longfellow's "Michael Angelo," published in 1885, Houghton, Mifflin and Company produced a small folio, the binding of which is obviously patterned after that of a Chinese book. But the printing is on every page, and the paper is so stiff that the book will not lie open. In the holiday edition which the same publishers issued in 1896 of Aldrich's poem, entitled "Friar Jerome's Beautiful

Book," they produced a volume in which the front folds were not intended to be cut open; but they outdid the Chinese by printing on only one of the pages exposed at each opening of the book, instead of on both, as the Chinese do, thus utilizing only one-fourth of the possible printing surface of the volume. In this case again the paper was stiff and the binding was full leather with heavy tapes for tying. A much closer approach to the Chinese book form was afforded by "The Periodical," issued by Henry Frowde, in the form which it bore at first. Here we have what may fairly be called a naturalization of the Chinese book idea in the occident. But let us see exactly what that Chinese book form is.

The standard book is printed from engraved wood blocks, each of which is engraved on the side of the board, not on the end like our wood blocks, and for economy is engraved on both its sides. Each of these surfaces prints one sheet of paper, making two pages. The paper, being unsized, is printed on only one side, and the fold is not at the back, as in our books, but at the front. The running headline, as we should call it, with the page number, is printed in a central column, which is folded through when the book is bound, coming half on one page and half on the other. There is always printed in this column a fan-shaped device, called the fish's tail, whose notch indicates where the fold is to come. It may be remarked in passing that the Chinese book begins on what to us is the last page, and that the lines read from top to bottom and follow one another from right to left. Each page has a double ruled line at top and bottom and on the inner edge. The top and bottom lines and the fish's tail, being printed across the front fold, show as black lines banding the front edge when the book is bound. The bottom line is taken by the binder as his guide in arranging the sheets, this line always appearing true on the front edge and the others blurred. The top margin has more than twice the breadth of the lower. After the sheets are gathered, holes are punched at proper distances from the back edge —four seems to be the regulation number whether the book be large or small, but large books have an extra hole at top and bottom towards the corner from the last hole. These holes are then plugged with rolls of paper to keep the sheets in position, and the top, bottom, and back edges are shaved with a sharp, heavy knife, fifty or more volumes being trimmed at the same stroke. A piece of silk is pasted over the upper and lower corners of the back. Covers, consisting of two sheets of colored paper folded in front like the pages, are placed at front and back, but not covering the back edge, or there is an outer sheet of colored paper with inside lining paper and a leaf of heavy paper between for stiffening. Silk cord is sewn through the holes and neatly tied, and the book is done—light in the hand and lying open well, inexpensive and capable with proper treatment of lasting for centuries.

What are the chief defects of the Chinese book from an occidental point of view? The most obvious is that it will not stand alone. Another is that its covers, being soft, are easily crumpled and dog's-eared. A third is that it is printed on only one side of the paper and therefore wastes space. All these objections must be admitted, but it may be urged with truth that our books, in spite of their relatively costly binding, do not stand alone any too well, and in fact this is a function seldom asked of books anyway. Its covers are soft, but this means at least that they are not so hard and foreign to the material of the book as to tear themselves off after a dozen readings, as is the case with so many of our bindings. There is no danger of breaking the back of a

Chinese book on first opening it, for it has no lining of hard glue. As to the utilization of only one side of the paper, it must be remembered that the Chinese paper is very thin, and that this practice makes it possible to secure the advantage of opacity without loading the paper with a foreign and heavy material. Moreover, the thickness of the pasteboard cover is saved on the shelves, and even if a substitute for it is adopted, it is in the form of a light pasteboard case that holds several volumes at once. Such a cover is capable of being lettered on the back, though the Chinese seem not to think this necessary, but put their title labels on the side. Really, the back of the Chinese book is to us its most foreign feature. It is a raw edge, not protected by the cover, and differs from the front only in consisting of the edges of single leaves instead of folds. It is in fact a survival from the days before the invention of paper, when books were printed on silk, the raw edge of which would fray and was therefore consigned to the position where it would have the least wear and would do the least harm if worn.

But there is no reason why, in Europeanizing the Chinese book, the corner guard should not be extended the whole length of the back and bear the ordinary lettering. With this slight difference the Chinese book would be equipped to enter the lists on fairly even terms against the prevailing occidental type of book, which has come down to us from the ancient Roman codex through the parchment book, of which ours is only a paper imitation. In "The Periodical," referred to, four pages instead of two were printed at once, or, at least, four constitute a fold. The sheets are stitched through with thread—they might, of course, have been wire-stitched—and then a paper cover is pasted on, as in the case of any magazine or paper-bound book. But in this process the beauty of the Chinese binding disappears, though the Chinese do the same with their cheapest pamphlets. In these days, when lightness and easy handling are such popular features in books, what publisher will take up the book form that for two thousand years has enshrined the wisdom of the Flowery Kingdom, and by trifling adaptations here and there make it his own and ours?

THICK PAPER AND THIN

SIR HIRAM MAXIM, the knight from Maine, prophesies that we shall change our religion twenty times in the next twenty thousand years. In the last two thousand years we have changed our book material twice, from papyrus to parchment and from parchment to paper, with a consequent change of the book form from the roll to the codex. Shall we therefore change our book material twenty times in the next twenty thousand years? Only time itself can tell; but for five hundred years the book has never been in such unstable equilibrium as at present; the proverb "A book's a book" has never possessed so little definite meaning. This condition applies chiefly to the paper, but as this changes, the binding will also change from its present costly and impermanent character to something at once cheaper and more durable.

The changes in modern paper have worked in two opposite directions, represented on the one hand by Oxford India paper, with its miraculous thinness, opacity, and lightness, and on the other hand by papers that, while also remarkably light, offer, as a sample book expresses it, "excellent bulk"; for instance, 272 pages to an inch as against 1500 to an inch of Oxford India paper.[1] The contrasted effects of these two

[1] Mr. Edison's projected substitute for paper, sheets of nickel, 20,000 to the inch, may indicate the book material of the future, but at present it is only a startling possibility.

types of material upon the book as a mechanical product are well worth the consideration of all who are engaged in the making of books.

Some of these results are surprising. What, for instance, could be more illogical than to make a book any thicker than strength and convenience require? Yet one has only to step out into the markets where books and buyers meet to find a real demand for this excess of bulk. Though illogical, the demand for size in books is profoundly psychological and goes back to the most primitive instincts of human nature. The first of all organs in biological development, the stomach, will not do its work properly unless it has quantity as well as quality to deal with. So the eye has established a certain sense of relationship between size and value, and every publisher knows that in printing from given plates he can get twice as much for the book at a trifling excess of cost if he uses thicker paper and gives wider margins. That all publishers do not follow these lines is due to the fact that other elements enter into the total field of bookselling besides quantity, the chief of which is cost, and another of which, growing in importance, is compactness. But it is safe to say that to the buyer who is not, for the moment at least, counting the cost, mere bulk makes as great an appeal as any single element of attractiveness in the sum total of a book.

This attraction of bulk receives a striking increase if it is associated with lightness. The customer who takes up a large book and suddenly finds it light to hold receives a pleasurable shock which goes far towards making him a purchaser. He seems not to ask or care whether he may be getting few pages for his money. The presence of this single, agreeable element of lightness at once gives a distinction to the book that appears to supplant all other requirements.

The purchaser does not realize that the same lightness of volume associated with half the thickness would not seem to him remarkable, though the book would take up only half the room on his shelves. He feels that a modern miracle in defiance of gravitation has been wrought in his favor, and he is willing to pay for the privilege of enjoying it.

Curiously and somewhat unexpectedly the results of neither extreme, thick paper nor thin, are wholly satisfactory in the library. The parvenu, who is looking only to the filling up of his shelves with volumes of impressive size, may find satisfaction in contemplating wide backs. But the scholar and the public librarian will grudge the space which this "excellent bulk" occupies. One single element in their favor he will be quick to recognize, the better space which they afford for distinct lettering. In a private library that is collected for use and not for show the thin-paper books are almost an unmixed blessing. They cost little for what they contain. Their reduction in thickness is often associated with a reduction in height and width, so that they represent an economy of space all round. A first-rate example of this is furnished by the Oxford India Paper Dickens, in seventeen volumes, printed in large type, yet, as bound, occupying a cubical space of only 13 by 7 by 4½ inches and weighing only nine pounds. A more startling instance is that of the novels of Thomas Love Peacock, which are issued in a pretty library edition of ten volumes. But they are also issued in a *single* volume, no higher nor wider, and only *three-fourths of an inch thick*. But it is at this point that the public librarian rises to protest. It is all very well, he says, for the private owner to have his literature in this concentrated form, but for himself, how is he to satisfy the eight readers who call for "Headlong Hall," "Nightmare Abbey," and the rest of Peacock's novels all at once? To be sure he can buy and catalogue eight single-volume sets of the author's works instead of one set in ten volumes, and when he has done this each reader will be sure to find the particular novel that he is looking for so long as a set remains; but the cost will naturally be greater. On the other hand, he welcomes equally with the private buyer the thin-paper edition of the Shakespeare Apocrypha, which needs only a third of the shelf space required for the regular edition, seven-sixteenths of an inch as against an inch and five-sixteenths. He also looks upon his magazine shelves and sees a volume of the "Hibbert Journal" with 966 pages in large type occupying the space of a volume of the "Independent" with 1788 pages in fine type, or again he sees by the side of his thin-paper edition of Dickens another on heavy paper occupying more than three times the lineal space with no advantage in clearness of type. By this time he is ready to vote, in spite of the occasional disability of overcompactness, for the book material that will put the least strain upon his crowded shelves. A conference with the booksellers shows him that he is not alone in this conclusion. Certain standard works, like the Oxford Book of English Verse and Webster's Collegiate Dictionary, have almost ceased to be sold in any but the thin-paper editions. Then there dawns upon him the vision of a library in which all books that have won their way into recognition shall be clothed in this garb of conciseness, and in which all that aspire to that rank shall follow their example. In short he sees what he believes to be the book of the future, which will be as different from the book of the present as that is from the parchment book of the early and middle ages of the Christian era, and as different in binding as it is in material. The realization of this vision will involve first of all a readjustment of values on the part of the public, an outgrowing of its childish admiration for bulk. But this change is coming so rapidly under the stress of modern conditions of crowding, especially in city life, as to reduce the vision from its prophetic rank to a case of mere foresight.

THE CLOTHING OF A BOOK

THE binding of a book is its most conspicuous feature, the part which forms its introduction to the public and by which too often it is judged and valued; yet the binding is not an integral portion of the volume. It may be changed many times without essentially changing the book; but if the printed pages are changed, even for others identical to the eye, the book becomes another copy. The binding is, therefore, a part of a book's environment, though the most intimate part, like our own clothing, to which, indeed, it bears a curious resemblance in its purpose and its perversions.

Human clothing is for protection and adornment. That of a book involves two other demands mutually so contradictory that bookbinding has always offered a most attractive challenge to the skill of the handicraftsman. The first demand is that the book when closed shall form a well-squared and virtually solid block, like the rectangle of wood from which its first predecessors were split, and shall be able to stand alone, unsupported. The second demand is that this same object, when open, shall lie flat at any point and display all its leaves in turn as fully, and far more conveniently, than if they had never been fastened together. Whatever may be true of other clothing, it is eminently true of a book's that the part which really counts is the part which is never seen. Only the ornamental portion of a book's covering is exposed. The portions which protect the book and render it at once firm and flexible are out of sight and unheeded by the ordinary reader. Hence the existence of so much bookbinding that is apparently good and essentially bad, and hence the perpetual timeliness of attempts like that of the present chapter, to point out what binding is and should be. The processes in bookbinding by which its different ends of utility and ornament are achieved are known under the two heads of Forwarding and Finishing.

Forwarding includes many processes, literally "all but the finishing." It is to forwarding that a book owes its shapeliness, its firmness, its flexibility, and its durability. Forwarding takes the unfolded and unarranged sheets as delivered by the printer and transforms them into a book complete in all but its outermost covering of cloth or leather. The first process is to fold the sheets and reduce their strange medley of page numbers to an orderly succession. This is assuming that there is a whole edition to be bound. If it consists of a thousand copies, then there will be a certain number of piles of folded sheets, each containing a thousand copies of the same pages printed in groups, let us say, of sixteen each. These groups of pages are called sections or signatures. They are now rearranged, or gathered, into a thousand piles, each containing the signatures that belong to one book. The edition is thus separated into its thousand books, which the collator goes over to see that each is perfect. Let us follow the fortunes of a single one. It is not much of a book to look at, being rather a puffy heap of paper, but pressing, rolling, or beating soon reduces it to normal dimensions, and it is then carried forward to the important process of sewing. This is the very heart of the whole work. If the book is badly sewed, it will be badly bound, though a thousand dollars were to be spent upon the decoration of its covering. There is only one best method of sewing, and that is around raised cords, in the way followed by the earliest binders. There are modern machine methods that are very good, but they are only cheap substitutes for the best. The cords must be of good, long-fibered hemp, and the thread of the best quality and the right size drawn to the right degree of tension without missing a sheet. After the sewing the end papers are put in place, the back is glued and rounded, and the mill boards are fitted. Into these last the ends of the cords are laced and hammered. The book is then pressed to set its shape, being left in the press for some days or even weeks. After it is taken out, if the edges are to be treated, they are trimmed and then gilded, marbled, sprinkled, or otherwise decorated. The head band — for which many French binders substitute a fold in the leather — is now added. It was formerly twisted as the book was sewn, but at present is too often bought ready-made and simply glued on. The book is now forwarded.

The business of the finisher is to cover and protect the work already done on the book, but in such a way as not to interfere with the strength and flexibility that have been gained, and, finally, to add such decoration as may be artistically demanded or within the means of the purchaser. If leather is employed, it must be carefully shaved to give an easily opening hinge, yet not enough to weaken it unnecessarily. This is a most important process and one that must be left largely to the good faith of the binder. If he is unworthy of confidence, his mistakes may long escape notice, but, though buried, they are doomed to an inglorious resurrection, albeit he may count on a sufficient lapse of time to protect himself.

The next and last process of finishing is that of the decorator, whose work passes out of the sphere of handicraft into that of art. His problem is no easy one; it is to take a surface of great beauty in itself, as of calf or morocco, and so treat it as to increase its beauty. Too often, after he has done his utmost, the surface is less attractive to the eye than it was at the beginning. He, therefore, has a task quite different from that of the painter or sculptor, whose materials are not at the outset attractive. This condition is so strongly felt that many booklovers leave their bindings untooled, preferring the rich sensuous beauty and depth of color in a choice piece of leather to any effect of gilding or inlaying. This initial beauty of the undecorated book does not, however, form an impossible challenge, as witness the work of the Eves, Le Gascon, and the binders of such famous collectors as Grolier and de Thou.

It may be well to consider more particularly what the problem of the book decorator is. Though perfectly obvious to the eye and clearly illustrated by the work of the masters, it has been sometimes lost sight of by recent binders. It is, in a word, flat decoration. In the first place he has a surface to work upon that is large enough to allow strength of treatment, yet small enough to admit delicacy; then, whatever in beautiful effects of setting, relief, harmony, and contrast can be brought about by blind tooling, gilding, and inlaying, or by rubbing the surface as in crushed levant, or variegating it as in "tree" or marbled calf, all this he can command. He has control of an infinite variety of forms in tooling; he has only to use them with taste and skill. There is practically no limit to the amount of work that he can put into the binding of a single book, provided that every additional stroke is an additional beauty. He may sow the leather with minute ornament like Mearne, or set it off with a few significant lines like Aldus or Roger Payne; all depends upon the treatment. If he is a master, the end will crown the work; if not, then he should have stopped with simple lettering and have left the demands of beauty to be satisfied by the undecorated leather. Above all, let every decorator stick to flat ornament. The moment that he ventures into the third dimension, or perspective, that moment he invades the province of the draftsman or painter. One does not care to walk over a rug or carpet that displays a scene in perspective, neither does one wish to gaze into a landscape wrought upon the cover of a book, only to have the illusion of depth dispelled upon opening the volume. Embossing is, to be sure, a literal not a pictorial invasion of the third dimension, but its intrusion into that dimension is very slight and involves no cheating of the eye. It has now practically gone out of use, as has the heavy medieval ornamentation of studs or jewels. In cloth covers, which are confessedly edition work and machine made, the rules of ornament need not be so sharply enforced. Here embossing still flourishes to some extent. But the decorative problem is essentially the same in cloth as in leather binding, and the best design will be one that triumphs within the conditions, not outside them. The machines and the division of labor have made sad havoc with binding as a craft. The men in America, at least, who are masters of every process and of all the skill and cunning of the early binders are few, and their thinning ranks are not being filled. Will bookbinding, in spite of a high economic demand, share the fate that has overtaken engraving, or shall we have a renascence of this fascinating handicraft and delightful art, to take its name from the present era?

PARCHMENT BINDINGS

THERE are certain things, the Autocrat informs us, that are "good for nothing until they have been kept a long while; and some are good for nothing until they have been long kept and *used.* Of the first, wine is the illustrious and immortal example. Of those which must be kept and used I will name three — meerschaum pipes, violins, and poems." May we present another representative of the class which gathers value with the "process of the suns," one as immortal and historic as wine and even richer in associations—the parchment book cover? In this case it matters not whether the object meets with use or neglect. So long as it is not actually worn to pieces on the one hand, nor destroyed by mold on the other, the parchment binding will keep on converting time into gold, until after a few hundred years it reaches a tint far surpassing in beauty the richest umber of a meerschaum, and approached only by the kindred hue of antique ivory.

Here is a table full of old parchment-bound books, ranging from a tiny twenty-fourmo, which will stay neither open nor shut, to thin, limp folios that are instantly correspondent to either command. Those that are bound with boards have taken on a drumhead quality of smoothness and tension, especially the fat quartos and small octavos, while the larger volumes that received a flexible binding resemble nothing in surface so much as the wrinkled diploma on yonder wall, with its cabalistic signature now to be written no more, Carolus-Guil. Eliot; but all agree in a tint over which artists rave, the color that gold would take if it were capable of stain. But there is no stain here, or rather all stains are taken up and converted into beauty. Dust, dirt, smudges, all are here, and each is made to contribute a new element of charm. Is the resultant more beautiful than the spotless original? Compare it with the pearly tint of the diploma, or turn up the folded edge of one of those flexible bindings and note the chalky white of the parchment's protected under-surface. The same three hundred years that have made over Europe and made English America have, as it were, filled in the rhythmic pauses between their giant heart-beats by ripening Dr. Holmes's wine and touching with Midas caress these parchment bindings!

It is surely a crime to keep such beauty of tint and tone hidden away in drawers or all but hidden on crowded shelves. Let them be displayed in open cases where all may enjoy them. But let us go softly; these century-mellowed parchments are too precious to be displayed to unappreciative, perhaps scornful, eyes. Put them away in their hiding-places until some gentle reader of these lines shall ask for them; then we will bring them forth and persuade ourselves that we can detect a new increment of beauty added by the brief time since last we looked on them. I once heard an address on a librarian's duty to his successors. I will suggest a service not there mentioned: to choose every year the best contemporary books that he can find worthily printed on time-proof papers and have them bound in parchment; then let him place them on his shelves to gather gold from the touch of the mellowing years through the centuries to come and win him grateful memory such as we bestow upon the unknown hands that wrought for these volumes the garments of their present and still increasing beauty.

LEST WE FORGET THE FEW GREAT BOOKS

ONE result of the stir that has been made in library matters during the last two generations, and especially during the latter, is the enormous increase in the size of our libraries. In 1875 the public libraries of the United States contained a little less than 11,500,000 volumes. In the five years from 1908 to 1913 the libraries of 5,000 volumes and over added nearly 20,000,000 volumes, making a total of over 75,000,000 volumes, an increase of 35.7 per cent. In 1875 there were 3682 libraries of more than 300 volumes each; in 1913 there were 8302 libraries of over 1000 volumes each. In 1875 there were only nine libraries containing 100,000 volumes or over. These were the Library of Congress, 300,000; Boston Public Library, 300,000; New York Mercantile Library, 160,000; Harvard College Library, 154,000; Astor Library, 152,000; Philadelphia Mercantile Library, 126,000; House of Representatives Library, 125,000; Boston Athenaeum, 105,000; Library Company of Philadelphia, 104,000. In 1913 there were in this class 82 libraries, or over nine times as many, including 14 libraries of 300,000 to 2,000,000 volumes, a class which did not exist in 1875.

Meanwhile the individual book remains just what it always was, the utterance of one mind addressed to another mind, and the individual reader has no more hours in the day nor days in his life; he has no more eyes nor hands nor—we reluctantly confess—brains than he had in 1875. But, fast as our libraries grow, not even their growth fully represents the avalanche of books that is every year poured upon the reader's devoted head by the presses of the world. To take only the four countries in whose literature we are most interested we find their annual book publication, for the latest normal year, 1913, to be as follows: Germany, 35,078 volumes; France, 11,460; England, 12,379; America, 12,230. But Japan, Russia, and Italy are each credited with issuing more books annually than either England or the United States, and the total annual book publication of the world is estimated to reach the enormous figure of more than 130,000 volumes. In view of this prodigious literary output, what progress can the reader hope to make in "keeping up with the new books"? De Quincey figured that a man might possibly, in a long lifetime devoted to nothing else, read 20,000 volumes. The estimate is easy. Suppose we start with one book a day—surely a large supposition—and count a man's reading years from 20 to 80, 60 years in all; 60 times 365 is 21,900. This estimate makes no allowance for Sundays, holidays, or sickness. Yet, small as it is—for there are private libraries containing 20,000 volumes—it is manifestly too large. But whatever the sum total may be, whether 20,000 or 2,000, let us see, if I may use the expression, what a one must read before he can allow himself to read what he really wants to.

First of all we must read the books that form the intellectual tools of our trade, and there is no profession and hardly a handicraft that does not possess its literature. For instance, there are more than ten periodicals in the German language alone devoted exclusively to such a narrow field as beekeeping. Such periodicals and such books we do not call literature, any more than we do the labors of the man or woman who supplies the text for Butterick's patterns. But they are printed matter, and the reading of them takes up time that we might have spent upon "books that are books."

But besides this bread and butter reading there is another sort that we must admit into our lives if we are to be citizens of the world we live in, contemporaries of our own age, men among the men of our time, and that is reading for general information. The time has long since gone by, to be sure, when any man could, like Lord Bacon, take all knowledge for his province—we can hardly take a bird's-eye view of all knowledge to-day. No amount of reading will ever produce another Scaliger, learned in every subject. To be well informed, even in these days of the banyan-like growth of the tree of knowledge, is to be a miracle of erudition. Most of mankind must be content with the modest aim which Dr. Holmes set for the poet, to know enough not to make too many blunders. In carrying out this humble purpose, that of merely touching elbows with the thronging multitude of facts of interest to the civilized man, we have a task great enough to occupy the time of any reader, even if he made it his vocation; and with most of us it must be only a minor avocation. The very books about the books in this boundless field, the compends of the compends, the reviews of the reviews, form in themselves a library great enough to stagger human weakness. Besides all this—in a sense a part of it, yet a miscellaneous and irrational part—come the newspapers, with their daily distraction. This is after all our world, and we cannot live in it and be absolute nonconformists. So we must submit to the newspaper, though it makes a heavy addition to our daily load of reading for information. But there is still another kind of necessary reading that I wish to mention before we come to that which ranks chief in importance.

The woman who takes out of the public or subscription library a novel a day is only suffering from the perversion of an appetite that in its normal state is beneficial. It is possible that her husband does not read enough for amusement, that his horizon is narrowed, his sympathies stunted by the lack of that very influence which, in excess, unfits his wife for the realities and duties of everyday existence. It came as a surprise to many to learn from Tennyson's "Life" that the author of "In Memoriam" was a great novel reader. But clearly in his case the novel produced no weakening of the mental fiber. President Garfield advised the student to mingle with his heavier reading a judicious proportion of fiction. The novel may rank in the highest department of literature and may render the inestimable service of broadening and quickening our sympathies. In this case it belongs to the class of the best books. But I have introduced it here as the most prominent representative of what we may call the literature of recreation. There is a further representative of this class that is peculiarly well fitted to bring refreshment and cheer to the weary and dispirited, and that is humor, which is often also the soundest philosophy.

If the reader does not at the outset make provision in his daily reading for the best books, the days and the months will go by, and the unopened volumes will look down upon him from his shelves in dumb reproof of his neglect and reminder of his loss. In truth it is all a matter of the balance of gain. What we rate highest we shall find room for. If we cannot have our spiritual food and satisfy all our other wants, perhaps we shall find that some of our other wants can do with less satisfaction. That we should neglect the material side of life for the spiritual I do not say. But for our encouragement let me quote another estimate of what may be accomplished by persistent reading, and my authority shall be the late Professor William Mathews, the essayist, an author whose graceful style bears lightly as a flower a weight of learning that would appall, if it did not so delight us. Says Dr. Mathews:

> Did you ever think of the sum total of knowledge that may be accumulated in a decade, or score of years, or a lifetime by reading only 10 pages a day? He who has read but that small amount daily, omitting Sundays, has read in a year 3130 pages, which is equal to six volumes of 521 pages each, enough to enable one to master a science. In five years he will have read 15,650 pages, equivalent to 30 large volumes, or to 60 of the average size. Now, we do not hesitate to say that 30 volumes of 521 pages each of history, biography, science, and literature, well chosen, well read, and well digested, will be worth to nine persons out of ten more than the average collegiate education is to the majority of graduates.

Our case for knowing the best books is, therefore, not hopeless. What we need for the achievement is not genius, but only a moderate amount of forethought and persistence. But who is there that has not tasted the joy of discovering a great book that seemed written for himself alone? If there is such a man, he is to be pitied — unless, indeed, he is to be congratulated on the unimagined pleasure in store for him. Discovery is not too strong a word for the feeling of the reader when he lights upon such a world-opening volume. He feels that no one else ever could have had the same appreciation of it, ever really discovered it, that he is

> the first that ever burst
> Into that silent sea.

Keats, in his glorious sonnet, "On First Looking into Chapman's Homer," has given the finest of all expressions to this sense of literary discovery.

Much have I travelled in the realms of gold
And many goodly states and kingdoms seen;
Round many western islands have I been
Which bards in fealty to Apollo hold.
Oft of one wide expanse had I been told
That deep-browed Homer ruled as his demesne:
Yet never did I breathe its pure serene
Till I heard Chapman speak out loud and bold:
Then felt I like some watcher in the skies
When a new planet swims into his ken;
Or like stout Cortez, when with eagle eyes
He stared at the Pacific—and all his men
Looked at each other with a wild surmise—
Silent, upon a peak in Darien.

To describe such accessions of spiritual vision we turn instinctively to the narratives of Holy Writ, to Pisgah and its revelation of the Promised Land, to the ladder at Bethel with its angels ascending and descending, and to the lonely seer on Patmos with his vision of a new heaven and a new earth.

But, questions a listener, do books ever really affect people like this? Most assuredly! We have only to turn to biography for the record, if we do not find living witnesses among our friends. It was said of Neander that "Plato is his idol—his constant watchword. He sits day and night over him; and there are few who have so thoroughly and in such purity imbibed his wisdom."

The elder Professor Torrey, of the University of Vermont, found his inspiration, as many another has done, in Dante. In his youth he preferred the Inferno; in his middle life he rose to the calm heights of the Purgatorio; and he used to say with a smile that perhaps the time would come when he should be fitted to appreciate the Paradiso. Highly interesting is John Ruskin's tribute to Sir Walter Scott:

> It is one of the griefs of my old age that I know Scott by heart, but still, if I take up a volume of him, it is not laid down again for the next hour.

Beside this we may place Goethe's testimony, also written in old age:

> We read many, too many, poor things, thus losing our time and gaining nothing. We should only read what we can admire, as I did in my youth, and as I now do with Sir Walter Scott. I have now begun "Rob Roy," and I shall read all his romances in succession. All is great—material, import, characters, execution; and then what infinite diligence in the preparatory studies! what truth of detail in the composition! Here we see what English history is; what an inheritance to a poet able to make use of it. Walter Scott is a great genius; he has not his equal; and we need not wonder at the extraordinary effect he has produced on the reading world. He gives me much to think of; and I discover in him a wholly new art with laws of its own.

Of Goethe himself Carlyle confessed that the reading of his works made him understand what the Methodists mean by a new birth. Those who are familiar with the speeches and writings of Daniel Webster realize the inspiration that he owed to the grandeur of Milton. His great rival, Calhoun, honored everywhere as a statesman, was known in his own home as "the old man of the Bible." It was the reading of the Bible that equipped John Bunyan to become the author of "Pilgrim's Progress." The novelists have not failed to recognize the influence of some single book on a human life. It was the accidental possession of a folio volume of Shakespeare—in Blackmore's "Lorna Doone"—that transformed John Ridd from a hulking countryman to a man of profound acquaintance with the world. And who does not remember Gabriel Betteridge, the simple-hearted old steward in Wilkie Collins's "Moonstone," who finds for every occurrence a text to counsel or console in his favorite "Robinson Crusoe"?

As the experience of Professor Torrey shows, different books appeal to us most strongly at different ages. Young men read Shelley, old men read Wordsworth. In youth "Hamlet" is to us the greatest of all plays; in old age, "Lear." I know of no more interesting account of the development of a mind in the choice of books than that presented in John Beattie Crozier's autobiographical volume entitled "My Inner Life." The author is an English philosopher, who was born and lived until manhood in the backwoods of Canada. He tells us how as a young man groping about for some clew to the mystery of the world in which he found himself, he tried one great writer after another—Mill, Buckle, Carlyle, Emerson—all to no purpose, for he was not ready for them. At this period he read with great profit the "Recreations of a Country Parson," which, as he says, "gave me precisely the grade and shade of platitude I required." But more important were the weekly sermons of Henry Ward Beecher. Of him Crozier says:

> For years his printed sermons were the main source of my instruction and delight. His range and variety of observation . . . his width of sympathy; his natural and spontaneous pathos; the wealth of illustration and metaphor with which his sermons were adorned, and which were drawn chiefly from natural objects, from his orchard, his farm, his garden, as well as from machinery and from all kinds of natural processes; his naturalism and absence of theological bias; his knowledge of average men and their ways of looking at things; in a word, his general fertility of thought, filling up, as it did, the full horizon of my mind, and running over and beyond it on all sides, so that wherever I looked he had been there before me—all this delighted and enchanted me, and made him for some years my ideal of intellectual greatness; and I looked forward to the Saturdays on which his weekly sermons reached me with longing and pure joy.

Later, in England, Crozier took up the works of the philosophers with better success. The chapter of most interest for us is the one on the group which he calls "The Poetic Thinkers"—Carlyle, Newman, Emerson, Goethe. Of these he places Goethe and Emerson highest. Indeed of Emerson's essay on "Experience" he says:

> In this simple framework Emerson has contrived to work in thoughts on human life more central and commanding, more ultimate and final, and of more universal application than are to be found within the same compass in the literature of any age or time, thoughts which rise to the mind as naturally and spontaneously when the deeper secrets of life are in question, as proverbs do in its more obvious and superficial aspects. . . . Nowhere, indeed, will you find greater penetration and profundity, or greater refinement and delicacy than in these essays (of Emerson). . . . After a lapse of ten or fifteen years . . . no increase of experience or reflection has enabled me to add or suggest aught by way of commentary on these great and penetrating observations on human life that is not either more superficial or less true. . . . Until Emerson is understood, no observer of human life making any pretension to originality can, in my judgment, consider his reputation safe, or his work free from the danger of being undermined by this great master of human thought.

If some scholar on whose judgment we relied were to speak in these terms of a book that was only to be read in Persian or Icelandic, how cheerfully we should bend ourselves to the task of learning these difficult tongues for the sake of the reward—the possession of the coveted thought. But the writings of Emerson are in our own language and accessible in the cheapest editions. If to us personally Emerson does not make this supreme appeal, there are other writers, all at hand, set apart from the great multitude of lesser spirits by that final weigher of human talents whom Bacon calls Good Fame. It is not that among the myriad volumes of a library we must painfully and largely by accident discover the few of highest worth—scanning each doubtfully as one searches for an unknown visitor in the crowd alighting from a train. No, the best books are the best known, the most accessible. Lists of the ten, the fifty, the one hundred best books are at our disposal, and, if they do not always represent final judgments, are near enough for practical purposes. The will to read the best books is all that we need to supply—the rest has been done for us. And is there anyone who turns with indifference from the high and free privilege of making the greatest spirits that have ever lived his bosom friends, his companions and counselors? If there be such a one, would that I might repeat to him more of that glorious chant in praise of books that has been sung by the wise of all ages, from Socrates to Gladstone. I have given a few of these tributes already; I will close with one from an unexpected source. Says Walt Whitman, in his "Democratic Vistas," speaking of the books that have come down to us from antiquity:

> A few immortal compositions, small in size, yet compassing what measureless values of reminiscence, contemporary portraitures, manners, idioms and beliefs, with deepest inference, hint and thought, to tie and touch forever the old, new body, and the old, new soul. These! and still these! bearing the freight so dear—dearer than pride—dearer than love. All the best experience of humanity folded, saved, freighted to us here! Some of these tiny ships we call Old and New Testament, Homer, Eschylus, Plato, Juvenal, etc. Precious minims! I think if we were forced to choose, rather than have you, and the likes of you, and what belongs to and has grown of you, blotted out and gone, we could better afford, appalling as that would be, to lose all actual ships, this day fastened by wharf, or floating on wave, and see them, with all their cargoes, scuttled and sent to the bottom.
>
> Gathered by geniuses of city, race or age, and put by them

in highest of art's forms, namely, the literary form, the peculiar combinations, and the outshows of that city, age or race, its particular modes of the universal attributes and passions, its faiths, heroes, lovers and gods, wars, traditions, struggles, crimes, emotions, joys (or the subtle spirit of these) having been passed on to us to illumine our own selfhood, and its experiences—what they supply, indispensable and highest, if taken away, nothing else in all the world's boundless storehouses could make up to us, or ever again return.

PRINTING PROBLEMS FOR SCIENCE TO SOLVE

THE book seems to have been regarded for hundreds of years—for thousands of years if we include its prototypes—as a thing apart, subject to its own laws of beauty, utility, and economy. But recently men have come to realize that the book has no special esthetic license, that what is barbarous art elsewhere is barbarous in the book; they also recognize that the book is within the domain of economics, that the invention of typography was primarily a reduction of cost, and that a myriad later processes, which make the book what it is to-day, are all developments of the same principle. What has not been so clearly seen is that in the field of utility the book is not independent, cannot impose conditions upon its users, but is an instrument strictly subordinate to human needs. The establishment of its efficiency has only begun when we have adapted it to the convenience of the hand and the bookshelf. The real tests of its utility are subtle, not gross, and are, in fact, beyond the range of ordinary haphazard experience. In this field popular judgment may be right or wrong; it offers merely an opinion, which it cannot prove. But here that higher power of common sense that we call science comes in and gives verdicts that take account of all the elements involved and can be verified. Rather this is what science has not yet done for printing, or has done only in part, but which we confidently expect it is about to do.

What then are some of the points that we may call in science to settle? We know surely that fine type, bad press-work, pale ink on gray paper are all bad for the eyes. But there are a host of other matters connected with printing, we may even say most matters, in regard to which our knowledge is either uncertain or indefinite. In respect to this whole range of practical printing subjects we want to know just what practice is the best and by what percentage of superiority. This quantitative element in the solution is of great importance, for when rival considerations, the esthetic, the economic, for instance, plead for one choice as against another, we shall know just how much sacrifice of utility is involved. The tests for which we look to science cover everything that goes to make up the physical side of the book. The tests themselves, however, are psychological, for the book makes its appeal to the mind through one of the senses, that of sight, and therefore its adaptedness to the manifold peculiarities of human vision must be the final criterion of its utility.

Beginning with the material basis of the book—paper—most readers are sure that both eggshell and glaze finish are a hindrance to easy reading and even hurtful to the eyes; but which is worse and how much? Is there any difference as regards legibility between antique and medium plate finish, and which is better and by what percentage? In regard to the color as well as the surface of paper we are largely at sea. We realize that contrast between paper and ink is necessary, but is the greatest contrast the best? Is the blackest black on the whitest white better, for instance, than blue-black on buff-white, and how much? Is white on black not better than black on white, and, if so, in what exact degree? Or is the real solution to be found in some other color contrast as yet untried? The very mention of some of these possibilities shocks our prejudices and stirs our conservatism to revolt in advance; yet, with or against our will, we may be perfectly sure that the changes which science finally pronounces imperative will be made.

Who can tell what is the normal length of line for legibility, or whether there is one, and whether there is an ideal size of type, or what it is? Are the newspapers, for instance, right as to length of line and the books as to size of type, as many suppose? Has each size of type a length of line normal to it? How is this affected by leading, or is leading merely of imaginary value? Is large type desirable for the schoolbooks of the youngest children, and may the type be made smaller, down to a certain limit, without harm, as the children grow older, or is there one ideal size for all ages? It is frankly recognized that in certain works, like editions of the poets, legibility may properly be sacrificed in some degree to beauty, and in certain reference works, again, to economy of space; but we should like to know, as we do not now with any exactness, what amount of legibility is surrendered.

It is easy, however, to see that one great battleground of controversy in any suggested reforms must be the design of the type itself. Here, fortunately, the English public starts with a great advantage. We have thrown overboard our old black letter with its dazzling contrasts of shading and its fussy ornament, and therefore can begin where the Germans must some day leave off. We have no accents or other diacritical marks, and in this respect are superior to the French also. We start with a fairly extended and distinct letter like Caslon for our norm, but even so the problem is in the highest degree complex and baffling. First, accepting the traditional forms of the letters, we must determine whether light or heavy, even or shaded, condensed or extended letters are the more legible, and always in what proportion. We shall then be in a position to decide the relative standing of the various commercial types, if such we find, that fairly well meet the conditions. It will also be obvious what changes can be introduced to improve the types that stand highest. By and by the limit of improvement will be reached under the traditional forms of the letters. It will next be the task of science to show by what modifications or substitutions the poorest letters, such as s z e a x o can be brought up to the visibility of the best letters, such as m w d j l p. Some of these changes may be slight, such as shortening the overhang of the a and slanting the bar of the e, while others may involve forms that are practically new. It is worth remembering at this point that while our capital letters are strictly Roman, our small or lower-case letters came into being during the middle ages, and many of them would not be recognized by an ancient Roman as having any relation to his alphabet. They therefore belong to the modern world and can be altered without sacrilege.

There will remain other problems to be solved, such as the use of capitals at all; punctuation, whether to keep our present practice or to devise a better; the use of spacing between paragraphs, words, and even letters; besides numerous problems now hardly guessed. Many of the conclusions of science will be openly challenged, but such opposition is easiest to overcome. Harder to meet will be the opposition of prejudice, one of whose favorite weapons is always ridicule. But the results of science in the field of printing, as in every other, are sure to make their way into practice, and here their beneficent effect in the relief of eye strain and its consequent nervous wear and in the saving of time is beyond our present power to calculate or even imagine.

PRINTING PROBLEMS FOR SCIENCE TO SOLVE

The world at the end of the twentieth century will be a different world from this, a far better world, we trust; and one of the potent influences in bringing about that improvement will then be traced, we are confident, to the fact that, near the beginning of the century, science was called in to solve those problems of the book that belong to the laboratory rather than to the printing office.

TYPES AND EYES: THE PROBLEM

OUR modern world submits with an ill grace to the nuisance of spectacles, but flatters itself that after all they afford a measure of civilization. Thirty-five years ago Dr. Émile Javal, a Parisian oculist, contested this self-complacent inference, believing the terrible increase of near sight among school children to be due rather to a defect than to an excess of civilization. He conceived that the trouble must lie in the material set for the eye to work upon, namely, the printed page. He therefore instituted a series of experiments to discover its defects from the point of view of hygiene. Being an oculist, he naturally adopted the test of distance to determine the legibility of single letters at the limit of vision, and he employed the oculist's special type. His conclusions cover a wide range. He decided that paper with a slightly buff tint printed with an ink tinged with blue was the most agreeable combination for the eye, though in absolute clearness nothing can surpass the contrast of black upon white. He held that leading is no advantage to clearness, and that it would be better to print the same words on the page in a larger type unleaded. He found the current type too condensed; this is particularly a fault of French type. But he favored spacing between the letters of a word, a conclusion in which he has not been followed by later investigators. He found shaded type a disadvantage and advocated a fairly black type in which all the lines are of uniform thickness. But most interesting are his conclusions regarding the letters themselves. He found that the eye in reading follows a horizontal line which cuts the words just below the tops of the short letters, the parts of the letters being indistinct in proportion as they are distant from this line. It is chiefly by their individuality on this line that letters acquire distinctness. But just here he found that an unfortunate tendency towards uniformity had been at work, flattening the rounded letters and rounding the square letters. In a series of articles he gives exhaustive studies of the various letters, their characteristics, and their possible reform.

These ten-point lines in Della Robbia of the American Type Founders Company include the principal elements of reform advocated by Dr. Javal, as well as others mentioned below

A few years later Dr. Cattell, now a professor in Columbia, but then an investigator in Wundt's psychological laboratory in Leipsic, made a series of studies on brain and eye inertia in the recognition of letters. Like Dr. Javal he found some alphabets harder to see than others and the letters of the same alphabet different in legibility. He saw no advantage in having a mixture of capital and small letters. He condemned shading in types and opposed all ornament as an element of confusion. He regarded punctuation marks as hard to see and proposed that they should be displaced, or at least supplemented, by spaces between the words corresponding to the pause in the thought or the utterance.

He tested the letters by their legibility when seen for a small fraction of a second through a narrow slit in a falling screen. Beginning with the capitals, he found that out of two hundred and seventy trials for each letter, W was recognized two hundred and forty-one times and E only sixty-three times, the former being much more distinct and the latter much less distinct than any other. Some letters, like S and C, were found hard to recognize in themselves, and certain groups of letters, such as O, Q, G, and C, were constantly confused with one another. Said Dr. Cattell, "If I should give the probable time wasted each day through a single letter, as E, being needlessly illegible, it would seem almost incredible; and, if we could calculate the necessary strain put upon eye and brain, it would be still more appalling."

In regard to the small letters he found a like difference in legibility. Out of one hundred trials d was read correctly eighty-seven times, s only twenty-eight times. He found s, g, c, and x particularly hard to recognize by reason of their form; and certain pairs and groups were sources of confusion. The group of slim letters, i, j, l, f, t, is an instance. He suggested that a new form of l, perhaps the Greek λ, should be adopted; and he advocated the dropping of the dot from the i, as in Greek. He made experiments upon the German as well as the Roman alphabet, but he found the former so bad that he could only advise giving it up altogether.

Somewhat later, in 1888, Mr. E. C. Sanford, now president of Clark College, published in the "American Journal of Psychology" an exhaustive study on "The Relative Legibility of the Small Letters." He studied simply the letter forms, to determine the order of legibility in the alphabet and the groups most liable to confusion, in order to discover what letters most need improvement and upon what clearness depends. He too employed a special type. He found the order under the distance test to be w m q p v y j f h r d g k b x l n u a t i z o c s e, and the order under the time test m w d q v y j p k f b l i g h r x t o u a n e s c z. It will be noticed that of the seven letters most largely represented in a full font of type, e t a i n o s, all fall in the last third of one or the other of these two groups, four are there in both groups, while e, the letter used most of all, stands at the very foot of the list in the distance group. Could there be any clearer call for the reform of our letters?

Mr. Sanford enters at length into the question of the points that help and hinder legibility and that should therefore be considered in reforming the shapes of letters. Enlargement of size and increase of differences are obvious aids to clearness. Simplicity of outline and concentration of peculiarity upon one feature are important elements of legibility. Even a letter of small size, like v, is brought into the first group by a combination of these two qualities. Serifs are necessary to prevent irradiation, or an overflowing of the white on the black, but they should be stubby; if long, they take on the character of ornament and become confusing. The letters g and a are complicated without being distinctive and are therefore continually confused with other letters. The c e o group of much used letters can be made less liable to confusion if the gap on the right of the first two letters is made wider and the line of the e slants downward as in Jenson. Another group, a n u, are confused together. To avoid this the top and bottom openings of n and u should be made as open as possible and the a should go back to the old script form a as in the Humanistic type. The letter s is a source of great difficulty, being either not recognized at all in the tests or confused with other letters. It will be remembered that Franklin greatly deprecated the giving up of the long ſ, and a return to this form is now suggested, care being taken, of course, to differentiate it from f, especially by carrying it below the line. The dot of the i is of no use when the letter stands alone, but it is an important element of distinctness in words like "minim." The dot, as Dr. Javal suggests, should be set on a level with the top of the l rather than on a level with the top of the t. A reduction of serifs would lessen the confusion of x and z and of s and z.

But it is unnecessary to trace these studies in all their minutiae. In the twenty-eight years that have followed the appearance of Mr. Sanford's article work along the same lines has been done by many investigators in various countries. Some of the conclusions that we have noticed have been sustained, others have been discredited. The most important conclusions of the investigators down to 1908 will be found scattered through the pages of Huey's "Psychology and Pedagogy of Reading," which appeared in that year. Such matters as the normal length of a line of print, the size of type appropriate to schoolbooks for children of different ages, the possibilities of future type design with reference solely to the reader's needs, are among the many subjects there set forth in an interesting fashion.

In all these studies one obvious subject of investigation appears to have been overlooked, and that is the actual types of everyday print. Do they vary greatly in legibility? Are some of them so bad that they ought to be rejected *in toto?* On the other hand, have the designers of certain types attained by instinct or by happy accident a degree of legibility that approximates the best to be hoped for? If so, can we trace the direction to be followed in seeking further improvement? To answer these questions an extended investigation was undertaken at Clark University in 1911 by Miss Barbara Elizabeth Roethlein under the direction of Professor John Wallace Baird. Her results were published by Clark University Library in January, 1912, under the title "The Relative Legibility of Different Faces of Printing Types." The pamphlet abounds in tables made clear by the use of the very types under consideration. The following are the conclusions reached:

TYPES AND EYES: THE PROBLEM

1. Certain faces of type are much more legible than other faces; and certain letters of every face are much more legible than other letters of the same face.

2. These differences in legibility prove to be greater when letters are presented in isolation from one another than when they are presented in groups.

3. Legibility is a product of six factors: (1) the form of the letter; (2) the size of the letter; (3) the heaviness of the face of the letter (the thickness of the lines which constitute the letter); (4) the width of the white margin which surrounds the letter; (5) the position of the letter in the letter group; (6) the shape and size of the adjacent letters. In our experiments the first factor seemed to be less significant than any of the other five; that is, in the type-faces which were employed in the present investigation the form of any given letter of the alphabet usually varied between such narrow limits as to constitute a relatively insignificant factor in the determination of its legibility.

4. The relatively heavy-faced types prove to be more legible than the light-faced types. The optimal heaviness of face seems to lie in a mean between the bold faces and such light faces as Scotch Roman and Cushing Monotone.

5. The initial position in a group of letters is the most advantageous position for legibility; the final position comes next in order of advantage; and the intermediate or internal positions are least favorable for legibility.

6. The size and the form of the letters which stand adjacent to any given letter play an important role in determining its legibility; and the misreadings which occur in the case of grouped letters are of a wholly different sort from those which occur in the case of isolated letters. When letters of the same height or of similar form appear side by side, they become relatively illegible. But the juxtaposition of an ascender, a descender and a short letter tends to improve the legibility of each, as also does the juxtaposition of letters which are made up wholly or chiefly of straight lines and letters which are made up wholly or chiefly of curved lines.

7. The quality and the texture of the paper is a much less significant factor than has been supposed, provided, of course, that

the illumination and the inclination of the paper are such as to secure an optimal condition of light reflection from its surface.

8. There is an urgent need for modification of certain letters of the alphabet.

Contrary to previous results with special types, these tests of commercial types represent the capitals as more legible, by about one-fifth, than the lowercase letters; but, in view of the much greater bigness and heaviness of capitals, the earlier judgment would seem to be supported so far as the letter forms of the two classes are concerned. The order of each class, taking an average of all the faces, is as follows: **W M L J I A T C V Q P D O Y U F H X G N Z K E R B S m w d j l p f q y i h g b k v r t n c u o x a e z s.** Considering only the lowercase letters, which represent nine-tenths of the print that meets the eye, we still have four of the most used letters, s e a o, in the lowest fourth of the group, while s in both sizes of type and in all faces stands at the bottom. The average legibility of the best and worst is: W, 300.2; S, 205.7; m, 296.8; s, 152.6.

The tests were by distance; the letters were all ten-point of the various faces; and the figures represent the distance in centimeters at which the letters were recognized. There is a satisfaction in being assured that the range between the best and the worst is not so great as had been estimated previously, the proportion being in the one case not quite 3 : 2 and in the other not quite 3 : 1.5. The following twenty-six widely different faces of type were studied:

American Typewriter	Century Expanded
Bold Antique	Cheltenham Oldstyle
Bulfinch	Cheltenham Bold
Caslon Oldstyle No. 540	Cheltenham Bold, Condensed
Century Oldstyle	Cheltenham Italic
Century Oldstyle, Bold	Cheltenham Wide

Clearface	Della Robbia
Clearface Italic	De Vinne No. 2
Clearface Bold	De Vinne No. 2, Italic
Clearface Bold Italic	Franklin Gothic
Cushing No. 2	Jenson Oldstyle No. 2
Cushing Oldstyle No. 2	News Gothic
Cushing Monotone	Ronaldson Oldstyle No. 551

Of these, omitting the boldface and italic types, as well as all capitals, the six best text types, ranging in average distance of recognition from 236.4 to 224.3, are News Gothic, Bulfinch, Clearface, Century Oldstyle, Century Expanded, and Cheltenham Wide. The six worst, ranging from 206.4 to 185.6, are Cheltenham Oldstyle, DeVinne No. 2, American Typewriter, Caslon Oldstyle, Cushing Monotone, and Cushing No. 2. The author says, commenting on these findings:

> If legibility is to be our sole criterion of excellence of typeface, News Gothic must be regarded as our nearest approximation to an ideal face, in so far as the present investigation is able to decide this question. The esthetic factor must always be taken into account, however, here as elsewhere. And the reader who prefers the appearance of Cushing Oldstyle or a Century face may gratify his esthetic demands without any considerable sacrifice of legibility.

To what extent these conclusions may be modified by future experiments it is, of course, impossible to predict, but they clearly point the way towards definiteness and boldness in the design of types as well as to a preference for the larger sizes in their use. All this, as we shall see in the next chapter, is in harmony with what experience has been gradually confirming in the practice of the last generation.

TYPES AND EYES: PROGRESS

THE late John Bartlett, whose "Familiar Quotations" have encircled the globe, once remarked to a youthful visitor that it was a source of great comfort to him that in collecting books in his earlier years he had chosen editions printed in large type, "for now," he said, "I am able to read them." The fading eyesight of old age does not necessarily set the norm of print; but this is certain, that what age reads without difficulty youth will read without strain, and in view of the excessive burden put upon the eyes by the demands of modern life, it may be worth while to consider whether it is not wise to err on the safer side as regards the size of type, even by an ample margin.

It is now some thirty-five years since the first scientific experiments upon the relations of type to vision were made in France and Germany. It was peculiarly fitting, we may remark, that the investigation should have started in those two countries, for the German alphabet is notoriously hard on the eyes, and the French alphabet is encumbered with accents, which form an integral part of the written word, and yet are always minute and in poor print exceedingly hard to distinguish. The result of the investigation was a vigorous disapproval of the German type itself and of the French accents and the favorite style of letter in France, the condensed. It was pointed out that progress in type design towards the hygienic ideal must follow the direction of simplicity, uniformity, and relative heaviness of line, with wide letters and short descenders, all in type of sufficient size for easy reading. In the generation that has succeeded these experiments have we made any progress in adapting print to eyes along the lines of these conclusions?

The printer might well offer in proof of such progress the page in which these words are presented to the reader. In the four and a half centuries of printing, pages of equal clearness and beauty may be found if one knows just where to look for them, but the later examples all fall within the period that we are discussing. It may be objected that this is the luxury of printing, not its everyday necessity, and this objection must be allowed; but luxuries are a powerful factor in elevating the standard of living, and this is as true of print as of food and dress. It must be confessed that an unforeseen influence made itself felt early in the generation under discussion, that of William Morris and his Kelmscott Press. Morris's types began and ended in the Gothic or Germanic spirit, and their excellence lies rather in the beauty of each single letter than in the effective mass-play of the letters in words. Kelmscott books, therefore, in spite of their decorative beauty, are not easy reading. In this respect they differ greatly from those of Bodoni,[1] whose types to Morris and his followers appeared weak and ugly. Bodoni's letters play together with perfect accord, and his pages, as a whole, possess a statuesque if not a decorative beauty. If the reader is not satisfied with the testimony of the page now before him, let him turn to the Bodoni Horace of 1791, in folio, where, in addition to the noble roman text of the poems, he will find an extremely clear

[1] The type in which this book is printed is a modern Bodoni, cut in Italy, and was chosen for its elegance rather than to illustrate the latest results in legibility of type design.

and interesting italic employed in the preface, virtually a "library hand" script. But no force has told more powerfully for clearness and strength in types than the influence of Morris, and if he had done only this for printing he would have earned our lasting gratitude.

Morris held that no type smaller than long primer should ever be employed in a book intended for continuous reading; and here again, in size of type as distinguished from its cut, he made himself an exponent of one of the great forward movements that have so happily characterized the recent development of printing. Go to any public library and look at the novels issued from 1850 to 1880. Unless your memory is clear on this point, you will be amazed to see what small print certain publishers inflicted with apparent impunity on their patrons during this period. The practice extended to editions of popular authors like Dickens and Thackeray, editions that now find no readers, or find them only among the nearsighted.

The cheap editions of the present day, on the contrary, may be poor in paper and perhaps in presswork, they may be printed from worn plates, but in size and even in cut of type they are generally irreproachable. As regards nearsighted readers, it is well known that they prefer fine type to coarse, choosing, for instance, a Bible printed in diamond, and finding it clear and easy to read, while they can hardly read pica at all. This fact, in connection with the former tolerance of fine print, raises the question whether the world was not more nearsighted two generations ago than it is now; or does this only mean that the oculist is abroad in the land?

It is recognized that, in books not intended for continuous reading, small and even fine type may properly be employed. That miracle of encyclopedic information, the

World Almanac, while it might be printed better and on a higher quality of paper, could not be the handy reference book that it is without the use of a type that would be intolerably small in a novel or a history. With the increase of the length of continuous use for which the book is intended, the size of the type should increase up to a certain point. Above eleven-point, or small pica, however, increase in the size of type becomes a matter not of hygiene, but simply of esthetics. But below the normal the printer's motto should be: In case of doubt choose the larger type.

A development of public taste that is in line with this argument is the passing of the large-paper edition. It was always an anomaly; but our fathers did not stop to reason that, if a page has the right proportions at the start, mere increase of margin cannot enhance its beauty or dignity. At most it can only lend it a somewhat deceptive appearance of costliness, with which was usually coupled whatever attraction there might be in the restriction of this special edition to a very few copies. So they paid many dollars a pound for mere blank paper and fancied that they were getting their money's worth. The most inappropriate books were put out in large paper, Webster's Unabridged Dictionary, for instance. At the other extreme of size may be cited the Pickering diamond classics, also in a large-paper edition, pretty, dainty little books, with their Lilliputian character only emphasized by their excess of white paper. But their print is too fine to read, and their margins are out of proportion to the printed page. Though their type is small, they by no means exhibit the miracle of the books printed in Didot's "microscopic" type, and they represent effort in a direction that has no meaning for bookmaking, but remains a mere *tour de force*. Quite different is the case with the Oxford miniature editions, of the same size outwardly as the large-paper editions of the Pickering diamond classics; these are modern miracles, for with all their "infinite riches in a little room," they are distinctly legible.

As regards the design of type, the recent decades have given us our choice among type-faces at once so beautiful and so clear as the Century Oldstyle, Century Expanded, and Cheltenham Wide. To those should be added Mr. Goudy's virile Kennerley. Still later have appeared, in direct descent from one of Jenson's type-faces, Cloister and Centaur, two of the most beautiful types of any age or country, and both, if we may judge by comparison with the types approved by the Clark University experiments, also among the most legible. Fortunately in type design there is no essential conflict between beauty and use, but rather a natural harmony. Already a high degree of legibility has been attained without sacrifice; the future is full of promise.

In respect to books, we may congratulate ourselves that printing has made real progress in the last generation towards meeting the primary demand of legibility. The form of print, however, which is read by the greatest number of eyes, the newspaper, shows much less advance. Yet newspapers have improved in presswork, and the typesetting machines have removed the evil of worn type. Moreover, a new element has come to the front that played a much more subordinate part three or four decades ago — the headline. "Let me write the headlines of a people," said the late Henry D. Lloyd to the writer, "and I care not who makes its laws." It is the staring headlines that form the staple of the busy man's newspaper reading, and they are certainly hygienic for the eyes if not always for the mind. While the trend towards larger and clearer type has gone on chiefly without the consciousness of the public, it has not been merely a reform imposed from without. The public prefers readable print, demands it, and is ready to pay for it. The magazines have long recognized this phase of public taste. When the newspapers have done the same, the eyes of coming generations will be relieved of a strain that can only be realized by those who in that day shall turn as a matter of antiquarian curiosity to the torturing fine print that so thickly beset the pathway of knowledge from the sixteenth to the nineteenth century, and, in the twentieth, overthrown in the field of books and magazines, made its last, wavering stand in the newspapers.

EXCEPTIONS TO THE RULE OF LEGIBILITY

SINCE print is meant primarily to be read, the first law of its being is legibility. As a general principle this must be accepted, but in the application certain important reservations must be made, all relating themselves to the question *how* the print is to be read. For straightaway, long-time reading, or for reading in which the aim is to get at the words of the author with the least hindrance, the law of legibility holds to its full extent—is, in fact, an axiom; but not all reading is long-continued, and not all is apart from considerations other than instantaneous contact with the author's thought through his words. It is these two classes of exceptions that we have now to consider.

Let us begin with an example outside the field of typography. On the first issue of the Lincoln cent were various sizes of lettering, the largest being devoted to the words which denote the value of the coin, and the smallest, quite undistinguishable in ordinary handling, to the initials of the designer, afterwards discarded. Obviously these sizes were chosen with reference to their power to attract attention; in the one case an excess of legibility and in the other case, quite as properly, its deficiency. Thus, what is not designed for the cursory reader's eye, but serves only as a record to be consulted by those who are specially interested in it, may, with propriety, be made so inconspicuous as to be legible only by a distinct effort. Cases in everyday typography are the signatures of books and the cabalistic symbols that indicate to the newspaper counting room the standing of advertisements. Both are customarily rendered inconspicuous through obscure position, and if to this be added the relative illegibility of fine type, the average reader will not complain, for all will escape his notice.

Again, we may say that what is not intended for ordinary continuous reading may, without criticism, be consigned to type below normal size. Certain classes of books that are intended only for brief consultation come under this head, the best examples being encyclopedias, dictionaries, and almanacs. As compactness is one of their prime requisites, it is a mistake to put them into type even comfortably large. The reader opens them only for momentary reference, and he can well afford to sacrifice a certain degree of legibility to handiness. The Encyclopædia Britannica is a classic instance of a work made bulky by type unnecessarily coarse for its purpose; the later, amazingly clear, photographic reduction of the Britannica volumes is a recognition of this initial mistake. The Century and Oxford dictionaries, on the other hand, are splendid examples of the judicious employment of fine print for the purpose both of condensation and the gradation of emphasis. One has only to contrast with these a similar work in uniform type, such as Littré's Dictionnaire, to appreciate their superiority for ready reference.

The departure from legibility that we have thus far considered has related to the size of the letters. Another equally marked departure is possible in respect to their shape. In business printing, especially in newspaper advertisements, men are sometimes tempted to gain amount at the risk of undue fineness of type. But no advertiser who counts the cost will take the chance of rendering his announcement unreadable by the use of ornamental or otherwise imperfectly legible letters. He sets no value upon the form save as a carrier of substance. In works of literature, on the contrary, form may take on an importance of its own; it may even be made tributary to the substance at some cost to legibility.

In this field there is room for type the chief merit of which is apart from its legibility. In other words, there is and always will be a place for beauty in typography, even though it involve a certain loss of clearness. As related to the total bulk of printing, works of this class never can amount to more than a fraction of one per cent. But their proportion in the library of a cultivated man would be vastly greater, possibly as high as fifty per cent. In such works the esthetic sense demands not merely that the type be a carrier of the alphabet, but also that it interpret or at least harmonize with the subject-matter. Who ever saw Mr. Updike's specimen pages for an edition of the "Imitatio Christi," in old English type, without a desire to possess the completed work? Yet we have editions of the "Imitatio" that are far more legible and convenient. The "Prayers" of Dr. Samuel Johnson have several times been published in what we may call tribute typography; but no edition has yet attained to a degree of homage that satisfies the lovers of those unaffected devotional exercises.

What, therefore, shall be the typography of books that we love, that we know by heart? In them, surely, beauty and fitness may precede legibility unchallenged. These are the books that we most desire and cherish; this is the richest field for the typographic artist, and one that we venture to pronounce, in spite of all that has yet been done, still almost untilled. Such books need not be expensive;

we can imagine a popular series that should deserve the name of tribute typography. Certain recent editions of the German classics, perhaps, come nearer to justifying such a claim than any contemporary British or American work. In more expensive publications some of Mr. Mosher's work, like his quarto edition of Burton's "Kasîdah," merits a place in this class. A better known, if older, instance is the holiday edition of Longfellow's "Skeleton in Armor." Who would not rather read the poem in this Old English type than in any Roman type in which it has ever been printed? The work of the Kelmscott Press obviously falls within this class.

The truth is, there is a large body of favorite literature which we are glad to be made to linger over, to have, in its perusal, a brake put upon the speed of our reading; and in no way can this be done so agreeably as by a typography that possesses a charm of its own to arrest the eye. Such a delay increases while it prolongs the pleasure of our reading. The typography becomes not only a frame to heighten the beauty of the picture, but also a spell to lengthen our enjoyment of it. It cannot be expected that the use of impressive type will be confined to literature. That worthiest use will find the field already invaded by pamphlet and leaflet advertisements, and this invasion is certain to increase as the public taste becomes trained to types that make an esthetic appeal of their own.

Ordinary type is the result of an attempt to combine with legibility an all-round fitness of expression. But that very universality robs it of special appropriateness for works of a strongly marked character. It is impossible to have a new type designed for every new work, but classes of types are feasible, each adapted to a special class of literature. Already there is a tendency to seek for poetry a type that is at least removed from the commonplace. But hitherto the recognition of this principle has been only occasional and haphazard. Where much is to be gained much also can be lost, and interpretative or expressional typography that misses the mark may easily be of a kind to make the judicious grieve. But the rewards of success warrant the risk. The most beautiful of recent types, the New Humanistic, designed for The University Press, has hardly yet been used. Let us hope that it may soon find its wider mission so successfully as to furnish an ideal confirmation of the principle that we have here been seeking to establish.

THE STUDENT AND THE LIBRARY

WHAT does a student of five and twenty years ago still remember of his college? My own first and fondest recollection is of the walks and talks, *noctes coenaeque deum*, with loved and honored companions, in the bonds of a friendship that can be realized only in youth, under the inspiration of a common intellectual purpose, and, one is tempted to add, in the atmosphere of college halls; next arise golden hours passed in the library; and lastly there come back other hours, not always golden, spent in the classroom. This is, of course, only to enumerate the three influences that are, or should be, strongest in a student's life: the society of his fellows, his private reading, and his studies. Of these three factors of culture the first and the last are fairly constant, but the second is apt to vary in the experience of any small group of students from the foremost place, as in the case of John Hay, to no place at all. It is of this varying element in the student's conduct of life that I have undertaken to write.

Unless student intercourse has an intellectual basis, such as reading furnishes, it has nothing to distinguish it from any other good fellowship and can hardly escape triviality. The little groups of students at Cambridge which included such members as the three Tennysons, Hallam, Spedding, Fitzgerald, and Thackeray, while they were no doubt jovial enough, were first of all intellectual associations, where

> Thought leapt out to wed with Thought
> Ere Thought could wed itself with Speech.

In such companionship men not only share and correct the culture which they have acquired in private, but they are stimulated to higher and wider attainment. The classroom at its best is hardly equal to a good book; from its very nature it must address an abstract average rather than the individual, while a good book startles us with the intimacy of its revelation to ourselves. The student goes to college to study; he has his name thence. But while the classroom is busied, patiently, sedulously doling him out silver, he discovers that there is gold lying all around, which he may take without asking. Twenty-five years after he finds that the silver has grown black with rust, while the gold shines on untarnished. Librarians are often besought for a guide in reading, a set of rules, a list of books. But what is really needed, and what no mentor can give, is a hunger and thirst after what is in books; and this the student must acquire for himself or forego the blessing. Culture cannot be vicarious. This is not to say that a list of books may not be useful, or that one set of books is as good as another, but only that reading is the thing, and, given the impulse to read, the how and the what can be added unto it; but without this energizing motive, no amount of opportunity or nurture will avail.

But, having not the desire to read, but only a sense that he ought to have it, what shall a student do? I will suggest three practicable courses from which a selection may be made according to the needs of the individual. The first is to sit down and take account of stock, to map out one's knowledge, one's previous reading, and so find the inner boundaries of the vast region yet to be explored. This process can hardly fail to suggest not merely one point of departure, but many. The second method is, without even so much casting about, to set forth in any direction, take the first attractive unread book at hand, and let that lead to others. The third course is intended for the student whose previous reading has been so scanty and so perfunctory as to afford him no outlook into literature, a case, which, it is to be feared, is only too common. We will consider this method first. Obviously such a student must be furnished with a guide, one who shall set his feet in the right paths, give him his bearings in literature, and inspire him with a love for the beauty and grandeur of the scenery disclosed, so that he shall become not only able to make the rest of his journey alone, but eager to set out.

Where shall the student find such a guide? There are many and good at hand, yet perhaps the best are not the professional ones, but rather those who give us merely a delightful companionship and invite us to share their own favorite walks in Bookland. Such a choice companion, to name but one, awaits the student in Hazlitt's "Lectures on the English Poets." Of the author himself Charles Lamb says: "I never slackened in my admiration of him; and I think I shall go to my grave without finding, or expecting to find, such another companion." And of his books Stevenson confesses: "We are mighty fine fellows, but we cannot write like William Hazlitt." In this little volume which the most hard-pressed student can read and ponder in the leisure moments of a single term, the reader is introduced at once into the wonderland of our English literature, which he is made to realize at the outset is an indivisible portion of the greater territory of the literature of the world.

Hazlitt begins with a discussion of poetry in general, shows what poetry is, how its various forms move us, and how it differs from its next of kin, such as eloquence and romance. He then takes up the poetry of Homer, the Bible, Dante, and Ossian, and sets forth the characteristics of each. In his chapter on our first two great poets, Chaucer and Spenser, he points out the great and contrasted merits of these two writers who have so little in common except a superficial resemblance in language. Hazlitt is fond of presenting his authors to us in pairs or groups. His next chapter is devoted to Shakespeare and Milton; and we may remark that, while the student is in no danger of forgetting the existence of Shakespeare, he is likely to need just such a tribute to the greatness of Milton as the critic here presents. The volume contains later chapters of great interest on Milton's "Lycidas" and "Eve." It is not necessary for us to mention here all the subjects treated; Dryden and Pope, Thomson and Cowper, Burns and the Old English Ballads are among them. In every case we are not tantalized with mere estimates and characterizations, but are furnished with illustrative specimens of the poems discussed. But the initiation into English literature which we receive from Hazlitt does not end with the authors of whom he treats directly. Resuming our figure of a landscape, we may say that he takes us through a thousand bypaths into charming nooks and upon delightful prospects of which he has made no announcement beforehand.

I spoke of reading and pondering his book in a single college term. But, while this may easily be done, it will be far more profitable for the student, as soon as he feels drawn away from the volume to some author whom it presents, to lay it aside and make an excursion of his own into literature. Then let him take up the volume again and go on with it until the critic's praise of the "Faerie Queene," or the "Rape of the Lock," or the "Castle of Indolence" again draws his attention off the essay to the poem itself. And as one poem and one author will lead to another, the volume with which the student set out will thus gradually fulfill its highest mission by inspiring and training its reader to do without it. If the student has access to the shelves of a large library, the very handling of the books in their groups will bring him into contact with other books which he will be attracted to and will dip into and read. In fact it should not be long before he finds his problem to be, not what to read, but what to resist reading.

Suppose, however, that the student finds himself already possessed of a vague, general knowledge of literature, but nothing definite or satisfying, nothing that inspires interest. He it is who may profitably take up the first attractive unread book at hand; but he should endeavor to read it, not as an isolated fragment of literature, but in its relations. Suppose the book happens to be "Don Quixote." This is a work written primarily to amuse. But if the reader throws himself into the spirit of the book, he will not be content, for instance, with the mere mention of the romances of chivalry which turned the poor knight's brain. He will want to read about them and to read some of them actually. He will be curious as to Charlemagne and his peers, Arthur and his knights, and will seek to know their true as well as their fabulous history. Then he will wonder who the Moors were, why they were banished, and what was the result to Spain of this act in which even his liberal and kindly author acquiesced. He will ask if antiquity had its romances and if any later novelists were indebted to Cervantes. The answer to the last query will bring him to Gil Blas in French literature and to the works of the great English romancers of the eighteenth century. Fielding will lead him to Thackeray, Smollett to Dickens, Dickens to Bret Harte, and Bret Harte to Kipling. If he reads Cervantes in English, he will have a choice of translations, and he will not fail to mark the enormous difference in language, literary style, and ideals of rendering between the three versions of Shelton in the seventeenth century, Motteux in the eighteenth, and Ormsby in the nineteenth. If, like many another, he becomes so interested in the great romance as to learn Spanish for the sake of coming into direct communication with his author, a whole new literature will be opened to him. Furthermore, in the cognate languages which a mastery of Spanish will make easy for him, a group of literatures will be placed at his command; and, while he began with Cervantes, who threw open for him the portals of the middle ages, we may leave him with Dante, looking before and after over all human achievement and destiny.

All this the student will not do in one term nor in one year, but he will have *found himself* in the library, he will have acquired a bond to culture that will not break as he steps out of his last recitation, that will not yield when time and distance have relegated his college friendships, with his lost youth, to the Eden or the Avilion of memory. And if afterwards he comes, with Emerson, to find the chief value of his college training in the ability it has given him to recognize its little avail, he will thus disparage it only in the spirit in which a more advanced student of an earlier day, looking back upon the stupendous revelations of his "Principia," likened them to so many pebbles or shells picked up on the shore of the illimitable ocean of knowledge.

ORTHOGRAPHIC REFORM

SELDOM have controversies brought out so much humor, on both sides, as that over the reform of English spelling, and few have excited so little interest in proportion to the energy expended. Both these results are due perhaps to the fact that the subject, from its very nature, does not admit of being made a burning question. Yet one has to look only a little way into it to see that important interests—educational, commercial, and possibly racial—are involved. Thus far the champions have been chiefly the newspapers for spelling as it is, and scholars and educators for spelling as it ought to be. But, in spite of the intelligence of the disputants, the discussion has been singularly insular and deficient in perspective. It would gain greatly in conclusiveness if spelling and its modifications were considered broadly and historically, not as peculiar to English, but as common to all languages, and involving common problems, which we are not the first to grapple with, but rather seem destined to be the last to solve.

As is usually the case in controversies, the chief obstacle to agreement is a lack of what the lawyers call a meeting of minds. The two sides are not talking about the same thing. The reformer has one idea of what spelling is; the public has another idea, which is so different that it robs the reformer's arguments of nearly all their force. The two ideas for which the same word is used are hardly more alike than mother of pearl and mother of vinegar. To the philologist spelling is the application of an alphabet to the words of a language, and an alphabet is merely a system of visible signs adapted to translate to the eye the sounds which make up the speech of the people. To the public spelling is part and parcel of the English language, and to tamper with it is to lay violent hands on the sacred ark of English literature. To the philologist an alphabet is not a thing in itself, but only a medium, and he knows many alphabets of all degrees of excellence. Among the latest formed is that which we use and call the Roman, but which, though it was taken from Italy, made its way back after a course of form development that carried it through Ireland, England, and Germany. This alphabet was originally designed for writing Latin, and, as English has more sounds than Latin, some of the symbols when applied to English have to do multiple duty; though this is the least of the complaints against our current spelling. In fact any inventive student of phonetics could in half an hour devise a better alphabet for English, and scores have been devised. But the Roman has the field, and no one dreams of advocating a new alphabet for popular use. Meanwhile, though the earliest English may have been written in Runic, and the Bibles which our Pilgrim fathers brought over were printed in Black-letter, still to the great English-reading public the alphabet of current books and papers is the only alphabet. Even this is a double alphabet, consisting as it does of capitals and small letters; and we have besides Italic, Black-letter, and Script, all in common use, all with double forms, and all differing greatly from one another. At best the Roman alphabet, though beautiful and practical, is not so beautiful as the Greek nor nearly so efficient for representing English sounds as the Cherokee syllabary invented by the half-breed, Sequoyah, is for representing the sounds of his mother tongue.

Let us now turn from the alphabet, which is the foundation of spelling, to spelling itself. Given a scientific alphabet, spelling, as a problem, vanishes; for there is only one possible spelling for any spoken word, and only one possible pronunciation for any written word. Both are perfectly easy, for there is no choice, and no one who knows the alphabet can make a mistake in either. But given a traditional alphabet encumbered with outgrown or impracticable or blundering associations, and spelling may become so difficult as to serve for a test or hallmark of scholarship. In French, for instance, the alphabet has drifted so far from its moorings that no one on hearing a new word spoken, if it contains certain sounds, can be sure of its spelling; though every one on seeing a new word written knows how to pronounce it. But in English our alphabet has actually parted the cable which held it to speech, and we know neither how to write a new word when we hear it nor how to pronounce one when we see it. Strangest of all, we have come, in our English insularity, to look on this as a matter of course. But Germans and Spaniards, Italians and Dutchmen, have no such difficulty and never have to turn to the dictionary to find out how to spell a word that they hear or how to pronounce a word that they see. For them spelling and speech are identical; all they have to make sure of is the standard pronunciation. They have done what we have neglected to do—developed the alphabet into an accurate phonetic instrument, and our neglect is costing us, throughout the English-speaking world, merely in dealing with silent letters, the incredible sum of a hundred million dollars a year.[1] Our neighbors

[1] See "Simplified Spelling in Writing and Printing; a Publisher's Point of View," by Henry Holt, LL.D., New York, 1906. About one half the expense falls within the domain of printing.

look after the alphabet and the spelling looks after itself; if the pronunciation changes, the spelling changes automatically, and thus keeps itself always up to date.

But this happy result has not been brought about without effort, the same kind of effort that our reformers are now making for our benefit. In Swedish books printed only a hundred years ago we find words printed with the letters *th* in combination, like the word *them*, which had the same meaning, and originally the same pronunciation, as the English word. At that time, however, Swedes had long ceased to be able to pronounce the *th*, but they kept the letters just as we still keep the *gh* in *brought* and *through*, though for centuries no one who speaks only standard English has been able to sound this guttural. In the last century the Swedes reformed their spelling, and they now write the word as they pronounce it—*dem*. German spelling has passed through several stages of reform in recent decades and is now almost perfectly phonetic. Germans now write *Brot* and no longer *Brod* or *Brodt*. It must be frankly confessed that the derivation of some words is not so obvious to the eye as formerly. The appearance of the Swedish *byrå* does not at once suggest the French *bureau*, which it exactly reproduces in sound. But Europeans think it more practical, if they cannot indicate both pronunciation and etymology in spelling, to relegate the less important to the dictionary. Much, to be sure, has been made of the assumed necessity of preserving the pedigree of our words in their spelling, but in many cases this is not done now. Who thinks of *alms* and *eleemosynary* as coming from the same Greek word? Scholars say that a complete phonetic spelling of English would actually restore to the eye as much etymology as it took away.

But the most deep-seated opposition to changing our current spelling arises from its association, almost identification, with English literature. If this objection were valid it would be final, for literature is the highest use of language, and if reformed spelling means the loss of our literature we should be foolish to submit to it. But at what point in the history of English literature would reformed spelling begin to work harm? Hardly before Shakespeare, for the spelling of Chaucer belongs to the grammatical stage of the language at which he wrote, and Spenser's spelling is more or less an imitation of it made with a literary purpose. Shakespeare and Milton, however, wrote substantially modern English, and they are therefore at the mercy of the spelling reformer—as they always have been. The truth is, Shakespeare's writings have been re-spelt by every generation that has reprinted them, and the modern spelling reformer would leave them at least as near to Shakespeare's spelling as our current spelling is. The poet himself made fun of his contemporaries who said *det* instead of *debt*, but what would he say of us who continue to write the word *debt*, though it has not been so pronounced for three hundred years? In old editions (and how fast editions grow old!) antiquated spelling is no objection, it is rather an attraction; but new, popular editions of the classics will be issued in contemporary spelling so long as the preservation of metre and rhyme permit. We still occasionally turn to the first folio of Shakespeare and to the original editions of Milton's poems to enjoy their antique flavor, and, in the latter case, to commune not only with a great poet, but also with a vigorous spelling reformer. Thus, whatever changes come over our spelling, standard old editions will continue to be prized and new editions to be in demand. But for the most part, though we might not readily understand the actual speech of

Shakespeare and Milton, could we hear it, we like to treat them as contemporaries and read their works in our everyday spelling.

Our libraries, under spelling reform, will become antiquated, but only a little faster than they are now doing and always have done. Readers who care for a book over ten years old are few in number and will not mind antiquated spelling in the future any more than they do now. The printer, therefore, must not flatter himself with the prospect of a speedy reprinting of all the English classics in the new spelling. English is certain to have some day as scientific a spelling as German, but the change will be spread over decades and will be too gradual to affect business appreciably. On the other hand, he need not fear any loss to himself in the public's gain of the annual hundred million dollar tax which it now pays for the luxury of superfluous letters. Our printer's bills in the future will be as large as at present, but we shall get more for our money.

It will indeed be to the English race a strange world in which the spelling book ends with the alphabet; in which there is no conflict of standards except as regards pronunciation; in which two years of a child's school life are rescued from the needless and applied to the useful; in which the stenographer has to learn not two systems of spelling, but only two alphabets; in which the simplicity and directness of the English language, which fit it to become a world language, will not be defeated by a spelling that equals the difficulty of German grammar; in which the blundering of Dutch printers, like *school*, false etymologies, like *rhyme*, and French garnishes, as in *tongue*, no longer make the judicious grieve; and in which the fatal gift of bad spelling, which often accompanies genius, will no longer be dependent upon the printer to hide its orthographic nakedness from a public which, if it cannot always spell correctly itself, can always be trusted to detect and ridicule bad spelling. But it is a world which the English race will some day have, and which we may begin to have here and now if we will.

THE PERVERSITIES OF TYPE

THAT searching analyst of the soul, Edgar Allan Poe, found among the springs of human nature the quality of perverseness, the disposition to do wrong because it is wrong; in reality, however, Poe's Imp of the Perverse is active far beyond the boundaries of the human soul; his disturbances pervade the whole world, and nowhere are they more noticeable than in the printing office. This is so because elsewhere, when things fall out contrary to rule, the result may often be neutral or even advantageous; but in the printing office all deviations, or all but a minute fraction, are wrong. They are also conspicuous, for, though the standard is nothing less than perfection, the ordinary human eye is able to apply the standard. These tricks of the malicious imp are commonly called "misprints," "printer's errors," "errors of the press," or, more impartially, "errata" or "corrigenda." In the first three names there is a tinge of unfairness, because the printer is by no means responsible for all the mistakes that appear in type. The author is usually partly to blame and may be chiefly; yet when he suffers a lapse of memory or knowledge, he usually passes it off as a "printer's error." Sometimes the author's handwriting may mislead the printer, but when so good a biblical scholar as Mr. Gladstone wrote of *Daniel* in the fiery furnace, there was no possibility that the single name could have stood in his manuscript for the names of the three men whose trial is mentioned in the *book* of Daniel. Even here the submission of proof fixes the final responsibility on the author. But, quite apart from the responsibility for them, the mistakes embalmed in type are among the most interesting of all literary curiosities.

Misprints—to use the handiest term—range in importance from the innocent and obvious, like a turned *a*, and the innocent and obvious only to the expert, like a turned *s*, to a turned *n*, which may be mistaken for a *u*, or the change or omission of a punctuation mark, which may involve claims to thousands of dollars. Even the separation of one word into two may reverse the meaning of the sentence, yet not betray itself by any oddity of phrase, as when the atheist who had asserted that "God is nowhere" found himself in print standing sponsor for the statement that "God is now here." The same trick of the types was played on an American political writer in his own paper regarding his pet reform, which he meant to assert was "nowhere in existence." The earliest printed books were intended to be undistinguishable from manuscripts, but occasionally a turned letter betrayed them absolutely. In the same way the modern newspaper now and then introduces an unintentional advertisement of the linotype by presenting to its readers a line upside down. Another trick is the mixing of two paragraphs, which sometimes occurs even in books. The most famous instance of this blunder is probably that which happened in the English "Men of the Time" for 1856, and which led to a serious lawsuit against the publishers. The printer had mixed the biographies of the Bishop of Oxford and Robert Owen the Socialist in such a way that Bishop Wilberforce was called "a sceptic as it regards religious revelation." The mistake occurred in locking up the forms. Doubtless both biographies had been approved by their subjects, but apparently no proof was read after the fatal telescoping of the two articles.

The last instance is an example of the patient waiting as much as the ingenuity of the Imp of the Perverse, but in pure ingenuity he is without a rival in mere human inventiveness. It certainly was a resourceful Frenchman who translated "hit or miss" as "frappé ou mademoiselle," and it was inspired ignorance on the part of a student assistant in a college library who listed "Sur l'Administration de M. Necker, par Lui Mème" under "Même, Lui," as if it were the name of the author of the book instead of being the French for "himself." But the Imp of the Perverse aims higher than this. He did not hesitate in an edition of the Bible published in London in 1631 to leave the *not* out of the one commandment from which its absence would be the most noticeable. This was much worse than leaving out the whole commandment, for it transformed a moral prohibition into an immoral command. The printer in this case was fined three hundred pounds, or five hundred dollars for each letter omitted. It is curious that the *same* omission was made in an edition of the Bible printed at Halle. A Vermont paper, in an obituary notice of a man who had originally come from Hull, Mass., was made by the types to state that "the body was taken to Hell, where the rest of the family are buried." In the first English Bible printed in Ireland, "Sin no more" appears as "Sin on more." It was, however, a deliberate joke of some Oxford students which changed the wording in the marriage service from "live" to "like," so that a couple married out of this book are required to live together only so long as they "both shall like." An orator who spoke of "our grand mother church" was made to say "our grandmother church." The public of Brown University was recently greatly amused by a local misprint. The president of the university is required by its ancient charter to be an "antipaedobaptist"; the types reproduced the word as "antipseudobaptist," a word which would be a very good Greek rendering of "hardshell." An express train at full speed having struck a cow, the report was made to say that it "cut her into calves." Sixty years ago the "London Globe" made the Registrar General say that the city was suffering from a high rate of *morality*. The ingenuity of our readers will supply the missing letter, as it also will the the true reading of the following passage which appeared in an English newspaper: "Sir Robert Peel has been out with a party of fiends shooting peasants." It was an easy but astonishing blunder made in German, in the substitution of "Mädchen" (girls) for "Mächten" (powers), according to which Bismarck was asserted to be "trying to keep up honest and straightforward relations with all the girls."

The Imp of the Perverse, when he descends upon the printing office, sometimes becomes the Imp of the Perverted. Here his achievements will not bear reproducing. Suffice it to say that in point of indecency he displays the same superhuman ingenuity as in his more innocent pranks. His indecencies are all, indeed, in print, but fortunately scattered, and it would be a groveling nature that should seek to collect them; yet the absence of this chapter from the world's book of humor means the omission of a comic strain that neither Aristophanes nor Rabelais has surpassed. Even as I write, a newspaper misprint assures me that typesetting machines are no protection against the Imp of the Perverted. Perhaps we may be pardoned the reproduction of one of the mildest of these naughtinesses. A French woman novelist had written: "To know truly what love is, we must go out of ourselves" (sortir de soi). The addition of a single letter transformed this eminently respectable sentiment into the feline confession: "To know truly what love is, we must go out nights" (sortir de soir).

Sometimes the Blunder Sprite deliberately pits himself against author, proof reader, and all their allies. The books printed by Aldus are famous for their correctness, yet a few errors crept into them, so much to the disgust of the great printer that he said he would gladly have given a gold crown for each one to be rid of them. The famous Oxford University Press is said to have posted up the first sheet of one of its Bibles, with the offer of a guinea for every misprint that could be found in it. None was found—until the book was printed. James Lenox, the American collector, prided himself on the correctness of his reprint of the autograph manuscript of "Washington's Farewell Address," which he had acquired. On showing the book to Henry Stevens, the bookseller, the latter, glancing at a page, inquired, "Why pap*a*r instead of pap*e*r?" Mr. Lenox was overwhelmed with mortification; but Stevens sent for a skillful bookbinder, who removed the objectionable *a* and with a camel's hair pencil substituted an *e* for it, so that the demon was conquered after all, but only through great trouble. How would it seem possible to reissue a printed book, copy it exactly, and yet make an atrocious blunder? The Type Spirit is equal to even this feat. The book was a mathematical one, full of formulae. It was not reproduced page for page, so it was perfectly easy for a signature mark to get printed and appear in the middle of a page mixed up with an equation, to the confusion of American mathematical scholarship. More tragic were the misprints in a work by the Italian poet, Guidi, which are said to have hastened his death. In an interesting volume by Henry B. Wheatley on "Literary Blunders," the Tricksy

Puck of the Press has revenged himself on the author for his attacks by smuggling in a number of misprints, among them one that he must have inspired in the mind of the author, the spelling "Bride of Lammermuir," which has no warrant in Scott's novel itself. In the same book is a reference to Shakespeare that diligent search fails to verify. Thus no knowledge or skill avails against the Kobold of the Case. The most baffling device of the imp is to cause a new error in the process of correcting an old one. This residuary misprint is one against which there is no complete protection. When General Pillow returned from Mexico he was hailed by a Southern editor as a "battle-scarred veteran." The next day the veteran called upon him to demand an apology for the epithet actually printed, "battle-scared." What was the horror of the editor, on the following day, to see the expression reappear in his apology as "bottle-scarred"!

Occasionally, however, the mischief maker takes a notion to improve the copy set before him The world will never know how often this has happened, for authors are just as willing to take credit for excellencies not their own as to lay on the printer the blame for their own oversights. In one of Artemus Ward's articles he had spoken of a starving prisoner as appealing for something to eat. The proof rendered it something to *read*. The humorist accepted the substitution as an additional absurdity. The French poet, Malherbe, once welcomed a misprint as an improvement on what he had written. There can be no doubt that, had there been no misprints in Shakespeare's quartos and folios, half the occupation of Shakespeare scholarship would have been lacking. Sometimes the original manuscript turns up—unfortunately not in Shakespeare's case—to confute some or all of the ingenious editors. A learned professor changed the word "unbodied" in Shelley's "Skylark" to "embodied," and some critics approved the change; but the poet's manuscript in the Harvard University Library makes the former reading clear beyond question. One might say that in these cases the Imp of the Perverse plants himself like a fatal microbe in the brain of the unfortunate editor. When that brilliant work, "The Principles of Success in Literature," by George Henry Lewes, appeared in the "Fortnightly Review," the expression "tilt stones from a cart" (used to describe careless writing) was printed with *l* as the first letter. When the chapters were reissued in America, the proofreader, warned by the presence of numerous other gross misprints, naturally corrected the meaningless "lilt" to the obvious and natural "tilt." This change at first escaped the attention of the American editor, who in the second edition insisted on restoring the original misprint and even defended his misjudgment in a note. It is worth adding that the Oxford English Dictionary takes the misprint as too obvious for comment and quotes the passage under "tilt."

The most daring feat of the typographic Angel of the Odd—to adopt another of Poe's expressions—is the creation of what Professor Skeat called "ghost words," that is, words that seem to exist but do not. A misprint in Scott's "Monastery" of "morse" for "nurse" was accepted without question by readers and gravely explained by scholars. Some of these words, of which there are scores, are due to the misreading of crabbed manuscripts, but not a few have originated in the printing office. It must be remembered that they make their way into the dictionaries. For another instance let the reader open Worcester's Dictionary to the word *phantomnation*. He will see it defined as "illusion" and referred to Pope. In Webster's Dictionary, however, he will learn its true character, as a ghost word formed by running together the two words *phantom nation.*

The printing of poetry involves all the possible mistakes liable to prose and, owing to the form of poetry, some new ones. Thus in Pickering's Aldine edition of Milton, two words of one line in "Samson Agonistes" are dropped down into the next, making the two lines of uneven length and very much hurting the emphasis. The three-volume reprint of this edition dutifully copies the misprint. In the Standard edition of Dr. Holmes's "Works" printed at the Riverside Press, in the unusual case of a poem in stanzas being broken up into a dialogue, the end of one speech, carried over to the following page, has been assigned to the next speaker, thus spoiling both the sense and the metre. The most extraordinary instance that has ever come under my eye occurs in a special edition of John Hay's "Poems," issued as a college prize volume and very elegantly printed at a well-known press. One poem has disappeared entirely except a single stanza, which has been attached to another poem with which it has no connection, not even agreeing with it in metre.

The list of errata, the printer's public confession of fault, is rather rare in modern books, but this is due as much to the indifference of the public as to better proofreading. When Edwin Arnold's "Light of Asia" took the reading world by storm, a New York reprint was issued, which we commend to anyone looking for classical examples of misprinted books. It averages perhaps a gross misprint to every page. Possibly extreme haste to beat the Boston edition in the market may have suggested dispensing with the proof reader. Of course a publisher who could so betray his customers would never offer them even the partial amends of a list of errata. Sometimes the errors are picked up while the book is still in press, and in that case the list of errata can be printed as an extension of the text; sometimes the best that can be done is to print it on a separate slip or sheet and either insert it in the book or supply it to purchasers. Both these things happened in the case of that early American book, Mather's "Magnalia." The loose list of errata was printed on the two inner pages of one fold the size of the book. In the two hundred years that have elapsed, most of these folded sheets have been lost, with the financial result that a copy of the book with them will bring twice as much as one without them, these two leaves weighing as much in the scales of commerce as the other four hundred. Sometimes a misprint establishes the priority of a copy, the error having been silently corrected while the sheets were going through the press, and thus adds to its value in the eyes of the collector. The extent of these ancient lists of errata staggers belief. Cardinal Bellarmin was obliged to issue an octavo volume of eighty-eight pages to correct the misprints in his published works, and there is on record a still huger list of errata, extending to one hundred and eleven quarto pages.

But we must not suppose that misprints began with the invention of printing. The name did, but not the thing named. In earlier times it was the copyist who made the mistakes and bore the blame. It is easy to see how in Greece and Rome, when one reader read aloud a book which perhaps a hundred copyists reproduced, a great number of errors might creep into the copies, and how many of these would result from confusion in hearing. Every copy was then an edition by itself and a possible source of error, calling therefore for its own proofreading. It is accordingly no wonder that the straightening out of classic texts is still going on. Had Chaucer, who wrote over a hundred years before printing was introduced into England, been able to read once for all the proof of his poems, he would not have had to write that feeling address to his copyist, or scrivener, with which we may fitly take leave of our subject.

> Adam scryveyne, if ever it thee byfalle,
> Boece or Troylus for to wryten nuwe,
> Under thy long lokkes thowe most have the scalle,
> But affter my makyng thowe wryte more truwe;
> So offt a daye I mot thy werk renuwe,
> It to corect, and eke to rubbe and scrape,
> And al is thorugh thy necglygence and rape.

A SECRET OF PERSONAL POWER

GREATER efficiency is the watchword of the hour. The pages of every technical and even educational magazine bristle with it. One is driven to wonder whether the principle does not require that in every printing office the word "efficiency" be stereotyped to save the cost of setting. We are told how one manager of a creamery saved annually the amount of his own salary to the company by having the dents in the supply cans pounded out and so getting more milk from the farmers. But though the lengths to which the insistence on efficiency is carried may sometimes provoke a smile, we have no inclination to disparage it; we realize that efficiency has far more than a mere money value to society; it is rather our purpose in the present paper to ask whether the efficiency man has ever thought to turn his searchlight in upon himself and discover whether he has not latent and unexpected powers that may be evoked to the great increase of his own efficiency.

We have nothing historically new to offer, though the principle we are to mention is practically unknown or at least unutilized. It is the great, controlling principle of Forethought, the application of which is far wider than thought itself, extending to all the functions of the soul and even affecting bodily energy and health. The action of Forethought is based on the fact that there is more to ourselves than we are aware of. We are not ordinarily conscious of our past lives, for instance, yet a supreme crisis, such as falling from a height, may make a man's whole past in an instant flash before him in review. Under sudden stress a man may develop powers of leadership or resolution that nobody could have foreseen and that he himself cannot account for. Our selves as we know them are, so to speak, only the top soil of our entire natures. Every conscious personality is like a farm in an oil district. It is underlain by an unrealized wealth that may never be brought to light. Some accident may reveal the treasure, but if the owner suspects its existence he may bore for it. To show how this boring may be done is one of the purposes of the present paper. But let us first assure ourselves further of the existence of this hidden fund of energy.

If in the early fifties of the last century a vote had been taken on the two men in America who ten years later would stand head and shoulders above their countrymen in position and recognized ability, it is probable that not one single vote would have been cast for a slouchy Missouri farmer or a shabby Illinois lawyer, certainly not for the former. Grant and Lincoln themselves would not have expected a vote. Yet their powers existed then, unrealized by their owners, and only needing the proper stimulus to bring them out. That stimulus was responsibility; and, great as their achievements were under this stimulus, neither man appears to have reached his limit; each apparently had still a fund of reserve power to be expended on yet greater occasions had they arisen. This is not to say that all men have an equal fund of unrecognized ability. The experiences of the great struggle out of which Lincoln and Grant came supreme are alone sufficient to show how unequal are men's endowments. A McClellan proves himself an unsurpassed organizer, but no fighter; a Burnside displays marked ability in leading fifteen or twenty thousand men, but beyond this number he fails disastrously. Neither Foresight nor any other device can *create* ability. A gallon can will hold only a gallon, no matter how carefully its sides are rounded. But in the case of any given man no one knows his capacity until he has had a chance to show it. His nature may hold only a pint, or, as with the men who have mastered great occasions with still unexhausted powers, it may seem like the horn which the god Thor tried to drain but could not, for its base was connected with the ocean itself. Not every man can hope to be called to a responsibility that shall bring out his latent powers; most of us, if we are ever to get the call, will first have to show the ability.

How can a man tap the unknown resources, be they great or small, of his unconscious self? The method here to be suggested has at least the merit of great simplicity. I have called it Forethought; it might perhaps as exactly be called Forewilling. The point is that this unconscious part of a man's nature is not out of his control; he can send word to it and direct it, even if he has to do so by a kind of wireless telegraphy. However mysterious this may sound, there is nothing mystical about it, neither is it something vague and indefinite, but a practice to be applied to actual cases in hand. Suppose a business man is trying to get an important contract, and is to have an interview on the morrow that will decide the question. Let him, before he falls asleep at night, go over the whole ground in his mind, set before himself clearly the thing to be done with the particular difficulties to be met, and let him *will* himself to meet those difficulties, to carry his case. Let him will that at that time he shall be cheerful and vigorous; and, having given these instructions to his unconscious self—which has perhaps been waiting years for just this chance to do its part in the common endeavor—let him dismiss the whole matter from his conscious thought and go to sleep. On awaking in the morning let him review the matter and again dismiss it from his mind until the occasion arrives. If he will do this faithfully, he may not succeed the first time in carrying his point, but he will certainly feel a great increase of power, and ultimately, if he persists in making his unconscious self an active partner in his life, he will find himself far more successful than he could have been while depending on a single side of his nature. The same principle will hold, of course, in a myriad cases; if we have to-morrow, or even at a later date, to plead a cause, to make an after-dinner speech, to write a report or an article, to learn a lesson, to entertain guests, to handle a difficult case of discipline, we have only to take this counsel of our pillow, to reënforce it with our first morning thought, and we shall find ourselves making a new record of success.

It is obvious that a principle so effective cannot be limited to the active or the intellectual life. If a man has a fault or a besetting weakness or sin, here is a way out of it. How long will a bad habit stand such an assault upon itself as the evening and morning practice of Forethought? One will actually feel the new force within him, like a gyroscopic stabilizer, holding him to his predetermined course. There is literally a world of hope for mankind in the application of this principle on its moral side. But the business of our article is with other applications and we must dismiss this, the greatest of all, with a mere mention.

If anyone questions whether this principle is true or not, the best answer will be to bid him test it. Though it be true universally, some people may not easily apply it, and some may not have the patience to subject themselves to such a discipline. But most will have no difficulty, and many will succeed well enough to inspire themselves to continue. Some, indeed, will say, and with perfect truth, that there is nothing new in this doctrine, that they have long known and applied it. The principle has doubtless been known for thousands of years, but it has certainly not been widely taken up by our race, which is curiously external in its notions of self-education and self-control. One American writer, the late Charles Godfrey Leland, a man of the most varied powers and accomplishments, has written in advocacy of it and gives us as his own experience that after the age of seventy he was able to do a greater amount of literary work, and with less fatigue, than ever before simply by calling in the aid of his unconscious self. If one were to read the lives and writings of eminent men with this principle of Forethought in mind, one would find numberless instances of its more or less unconscious practice. The best scholar in my own class, for instance, applied it to his studies. Does anyone suppose that the old Puritan's sweetening of his mind with a little Calvin before he went to bed was without its effect on his devotion to Calvinism? Erasmus, the wittiest of scholars, writing nearly four hundred years ago to his special friend, Christian of Lubeck, recommends the practice both of the evening instruction and the morning review as something that he himself has followed from his childhood; and we cannot doubt that in it he reveals one of the secrets of his world-wide influence. He says to his youthful friend: "A little before you go to sleep read something choice and worth remembering, and think it over until you fall asleep. When you awake in the morning make yourself give an account of it." Though this is clearly an application of the principle to study and the strengthening of the memory, experiment will show that the potency of Forethought is not limited to the memory or the intellect in general, but applies to man's entire nature and equally to the least and the greatest of its concerns.

INDEX

INDEX

INDEX

INDEX

INDEX

INDEX

INDEX

INDEX

INDEX

INDEX

INDEX

INDEX

INDEX

INDEX

INDEX